Straws in the Wind

Straws in the Wind

Medieval Urban Environmental Law— The Case of Northern Italy

Ronald Edward Zupko
Robert Anthony Laures

WestviewPress
A Division of HarperCollins*Publishers*

To

human concerns,

past and present

Copyright 1996 by Westview Press, Inc., A Division of HarperCollins Publishers, Inc.

Published in 1996 in the United States of America by Westview Press, Inc., 5500 Central Avenue, Boulder, Colorado 80301-2877, and in the United Kingdom by Westview Press, 12 Hid's Copse Road, Cumnor Hill, Oxford OX2 9JJ

Library of Congress Cataloging-in-Publication Data
Zupko, Ronald Edward.
    Straws in the wind : medieval urban environmental law—the case of northern Italy / Ronald Edward Zupko and Robert Anthony Laures.
        p.   cm.
    Includes bibliographical references and index.
    ISBN 0-8133-2971-X.—ISBN 0-8133-2972-8 (pbk.)
    1. Environmental law—Italy—History.   2. Refuse and refuse disposal—Law and legislation—Italy—History.   3. Environmental management—Italy—History.   4. Urban ecology—Italy—History.
5. Urban health—Italy—History.   I. Laures, Robert Anthony.
II. Title
KKH3127.Z87   1996
334.45'046—dc20
[344.50446]   96-12155
                                                                               CIP

The paper used in this publication meets the requirements of the American National Standard for Permanence of Paper for Printed Library Materials Z39.48-1984.

10   9   8   7   6   5   4   3   2   1

Contents

Acknowledgments

Our thanks go to many individuals and organizations for their assistance and generosity during the research and production of this book. We extend our sincere appreciation to the National Endowment for the Humanities and to Professor Jeffrey Burton Russell of the University of California at Santa Barbara. Much of the research underlying the contemporary philosophical, religious, and legal background that is crucial to the chapters here that relate to the elites' visions of the ideal city, urban quality of life, and the local environment was done during the 1993 summer institute entitled "Late Antique and Medieval Conceptions of Heaven."

Our research for more than a decade into the numerous statute collections, law codes, and histories of the medieval Italian cities whose environmental legislation forms the basis for this work could not have been accomplished without the deeply appreciated assistance of the interlibrary loan departments of the libraries of Marquette University, the University of Wisconsin at Milwaukee, the University of Wisconsin at Madison, Stanford University, the University of California at Santa Barbara, and the Northern and Southern Regional Library Depositories of the University of California.

Last, we must laud our research assistant, Kathy Callahan, for her long hours of patient and professional work, and the many people whose support and patience during the research and writing of this work sustained our efforts.

Ronald Edward Zupko and Robert Anthony Laures
Milwaukee, Wisconsin

Introduction

The environmental activists of the early 1960s and 1970s joyfully proclaimed to the world their love of the earth and the environment. Television screens were filled with the brilliantly colored images of happy, smiling young people in exotic dress and long flowing hair proclaiming their oneness with creation and their devotion to peace and love. They were vital, energetic, and positive—a driving engine for environmental change and a hallmark of the era.

The final decade of the twentieth century stands witness to a more mature environmental movement, perhaps less flamboyant, but certainly more purposeful. The contemporary desire for clean air and water, for the protection of limited resources, and for the renewal of endangered flora and fauna is often depicted as a modern phenomenon, the product of the enlightened twentieth century. Environmental awareness is portrayed as a thoroughly modern movement, arising out of the tumult of a half-century of war and depression like some Venus given birth in the crashing surf of a Mediterranean shore.

Is this, however, an accurate assessment of the origins of human concern for the environment and endangered resources? In the present study, we present evidence that human beings have been interested in the quality of the environment for almost as long as there are written records available. Men and women have long deemed it their responsibility to tend to the environment and the world about them. The literature on the subject contains innumerable references to their concern for the earth and to their efforts to produce a suitable quality of life in the context of both rural and urban settings. Their desire to create a dependable agricultural resource base, to preserve plants and animals, to tame the excesses of wild rivers and the effects of tidal flows on coastal lowlands, and to enhance the livability of urban environments are chronicled in the earliest extant examples of secular and sacred literature.

1

Examples of environmental awareness and concern abound in classical literature. Greek philosophers routinely speculated about the role of the human race in creation. Men and women were not conceived of as being mere consumers of the fruits and products of the earth but rather were seen as active participants in the completion of the creation of the world. They had a clearly defined responsibility and role in perfecting the earthly environment. Although individual thinkers might have differed on the role of humans or the extent of their responsibility for the world in which they lived, there was substantial agreement that the human race was the active agent for positive change in the environment.

The Judeo-Christian tradition reflected a similar belief structure. Human beings were still conceived of as being responsible for the earth in partnership with a monotheistic deity. Whereas Greek and Roman thinkers were more comfortable with deities that were often impersonal, remote, indifferent, or simply unconcerned with the human condition, the writers of the Jewish Old Testament tended to perceive God as a personal being genuinely interested in the creation and in the creatures to whom he gave existence. There was a stronger perception that humans and God were engaged in a joint venture designed to complete the divine act of creation. Humankind would work alongside the Creator to perfect creation, as an apprentice toils alongside the master craftsman. There was, thus, a plan, a desired outcome toward which all creation was directed.

The authors of the Old Testament had a reasonably consistent vision of the appearance of the finished product of creation. The image of a pastoral "land of milk and honey," given form, appearance, and consistency in the Book of Psalms and other texts, lent substance and reality to the goal of human endeavor. Men and women were not striving for some nebulous, formless intellectual concept of the ideal world. The Old Testament provided a clear, distinctive vision of a delightful pastoral environment that was thoroughly grounded in the real world of human experience and aspirations.

The writers of the New Testament and the early Christian era were direct heirs to this tradition and, in many ways, acted to enlarge upon it and to redirect its evolution. These writers lived in a physical environment that was considerably more urbanized and sophisticated than that of their Old Testament predecessors, a circumstance that caused the evolving tradition to be more concerned about the city and its ideal environment. Influenced by Christian thinkers, these writers had to face the reality of their perception of the sinfulness and depravity of contemporary urban life and the spiritual thrust of the mind and spirit into the next world;

they therefore developed a marked ambivalence toward the vision of the city. On the one hand, some of these writers wrote of gleaming cities built upon heights and decorated with brilliant fiery swaths of color, precious stones, and gems. They saw the earth as a "planned abode," whose continuing development was directed by an "Artisan God." On the other hand, some authorities, such as Augustine of Hippo (354–430 C.E.), who were frustrated with the lifestyle of the cities and the faltering Roman imperial system and anticipated the Second Coming and the approaching end of the world, tried to focus the minds and hearts of their readers and disciples upon the afterlife. But even these writers realized that they still had to live in the world and that they had some obligation to bring the Divine Plan to its fulfillment.

With the passing of the first millennium, the resurgence of urban life, the beginnings of the Commercial Revolution, and the extension of the "frontiers" of western and eastern Europe by monastic and military orders, medieval writers once again took up a more optimistic approach toward human life and the natural world. The notion that the human race was responsible for the completion of creation through the extension of agriculture into the wild forests and marshlands provided an intellectual and philosophical basis for the planting of thriving monastic establishments on carefully selected sites chosen for the suitability of their environments. At about the same time, the growth and ordered development of cities became a socially acceptable and philosophically supported endeavor. Indeed, Thomas of Aquinas wrote a work entitled *On Kingship: To the King of Cyprus,* in which he provided a blueprint for the enlightened ruler to follow in the creation of a new town; in many ways, this document was a summary of contemporary thought regarding the ideal urban environment. The "fantasy literature" of the day, as well as the more serious works penned by pilgrims and other more worldwide travelers such as Marco Polo, provided guides to the beautification and decoration of the ideal city. Thus, in the early centuries of the second millennium, a complete series of environmental guides based on contemporary technology was available for urban planners and monastic leaders, who thus had both the intellectual foundation and the conceptual models necessary to create towns and agricultural developments possessing ideal environments.

During the early centuries of the second millennium, the cities of central and northern Italy were in an excellent position to exploit this knowledge base. The collapse of Roman imperial administration on the Italian peninsula during the fifth century had a profound effect on Roman municipal government. In all too many instances, it simply ceased to exist; in those towns that remained, Roman administrative practices faded to mere vestiges of their former vigor or were usurped by barbarian invaders or ecclesiastical appointees who tended to center the remaining municipal services around the local markets or church squares. Lacking economic and military power, these towns were the frequent prey of marauding warlords, migratory peoples, or grasping kings and their generals, all of whom sought opportunities to loot, plunder, and subjugate.

Around the year 1000, a gradual economic and commercial revival began to take place on the Italian mainland, with the greatest impact occurring in the northern and central regions. This revival produced disposable financial resources for increasing numbers of successful craftsmen, merchants, and entrepreneurs. The newly enriched classes began to demand political power commensurate with their wealth, status, and contribution to their communities. When their demands for a share of the governance in their towns were denied by the entrenched ecclesiastical and imperial governing castes, they then organized themselves into political and military pressure groups to resist, and eventually supplant, the older ruling classes. Thus freed of the restraints imposed by extramural overlords, the townspeople began to develop the skills necessary for directing their own destinies and began to implement political, social, economic, and military institutions suited to the needs of their particular towns.

A unique series of historical coincidences had enabled the towns of the Lombard Plain to unite and declare their independence of pope and emperor. This independence allowed for the rediscovery and redevelopment of local municipal institutions. These institutions tended to be innovative because they were not imposed by a centralizing authority but rather were dictated by local needs. And they represented an amalgamation of old half-remembered relics of the Roman imperial administrative code, ingeniously configured innovations resulting from the clash of barbarian and indigenous Italian cultures, the new knowledge engendered by the cross-cultural contacts of merchants and crusaders traveling to and from the Near East, and the impositions of various external overlords. As the new municipal institutions took hold in the towns and cities, they were further revised and reformed to meet the changed circumstances of communal, signorial, and other evolving forms of regional government.

The new wealth and power that resided in the expanding towns spawned a new class of strongmen, who then acted to consolidate regional associations of towns. These regional overlords, or *signori,* were able to establish periods of relative peace and security during which there were economic surpluses sufficient to fund cultural and artistic revivals and municipal beautification projects. By the fifteenth century, a number of these regional *signoria* flourished and were so effective that even Venice found it expedient to turn its attention away from its overseas commercial ventures in order to concentrate on the creation of its own mainland-based empire, at the expense of other regional overlords.

It was under the hegemony of these regional overlords and republics that the medieval movement and awareness of the environment reached its highest expression. Environmental law in its most rudimentary forms can be detected in Italian municipal law codes as early as the eleventh and twelfth centuries. Impelled by increasingly distinct visions of the ideal city derived from the secular and sacred literature, the town elites realized early on that their visions of their towns and their aspirations for a particular quality of life would never be implemented without the force of law. Human nature and the impact of industrial and commercial development required more than the best wishes of good men to insure that the requirements of environmental quality standards were attained in the face of sloth and avarice. Municipal statutes, frequently revised, reformulated, and expanded, became the primary focus for the program of environmental reform and control in the medieval city and involved the entire community on a daily basis. The law bound everyone, was known to everyone in one way or another, and was directed to the specific objectives and goals of the ruling classes. And these laws, preserved in municipal archives scattered throughout central and northern Italy, provide the modern historian with the blueprints for the birth and evolution of the medieval environmental movement.

Northern and central Italy offer an ideal venue for this study not only because of the multitude of statute collections that have been preserved in usable form but also because the towns in these regions acquired sufficient wealth, power, and freedom to be the laboratories for the growth and development of municipal law. Furthermore, the lessons learned in the palaces and councils of these influential urban areas were common knowledge by the time many of the towns of northern Europe began to approach the levels of affluence and influence already attained by these Italian municipalities. The lessons learned and the approach developed by the Italian elites before and during the Renaissance were carried by scholars, ecclesiastics, and politicians into continental European and English cities, where they were absorbed and refined to meet the particular needs of those local environments. These ideas were, in turn, further refined prior to their transmission to the newly transplanted European towns and colonies in the New World.

* * *

This text is intended for the use of undergraduates, graduates, and the general public. Although we have sought to present a clear picture of the response of medieval urban elites to concerns regarding the environment and the quality of life within their towns, we also wish to express certain explicit caveats regarding the scope and purpose of this study. To begin with, the scope of the study is limited to a number of the smaller towns and cities of northern and north-central Italy between 1000 and 1750, and this research is based upon the regional statutes produced there within this time frame. We do not intend this study to be an exhaustive environmental history of the Mediterranean basin, continental Europe, or any other large-scale region in this era. Rather, the subject of interest here is activity within a microcosm—the reponse within northern Italy to the environmental issues facing those people and their leaders.

Furthermore, the focus of the study was not extended to treat all of the political, economic, social, or cultural aspects of the environmental movement of medieval Italy. Rather, we have limited the scope of our study to representative statute collections in northern and north-central Italy in an effort to determine how local officials in the smaller towns and cities of this region used the law to regulate the environment and the quality of life within their town walls. We were most particularly interested in the local response, rather than the regional response, to these concerns. The intention, within this rather limited context, was to gauge a response that was relatively free of larger regional, imperial, or papal influences in order to understand what the citizens of these smaller towns wanted to accomplish within the spheres of their own towns. The law codes were selected as the raw material of the study because we believe that the statutes enacted by the urban elites represent a true response to the environmental concerns of the urban population. Unlike chronicles, local histories, and other works penned under the auspices of aristocratic or ecclesiastical patronage, these statutes represent a pragmatic, perhaps political or economic, approach to the resolution of real urban concerns. These documents do not resemble the paid works of authors or poets, whose livelihood depended on the favor of their patrons; rather, they are realistic, legalistic, political responses to the real concerns facing politicians and citizens enmeshed in the daily conduct of business, family life, and politics.

We have had the opportunity to study representative statute collections of a number of medieval Italian cities, the most important of which are the following: Bassano, Bergamo, Bologna, Brescia, Cremona, Ferrara,

Florence, Lucca, Milan, Orvieto, Padua, Piacenza, Piran, Pisa, Pistoia, Ravenna, Rome, Siena, Spoleto, Venice, and Verona. The focus of this study is the purely local response of the municipal authorities of the smaller Italian towns to concerns relating to the quality of life and the environment in their towns as reflected in their law codes. Thus, the concerns considered herein are mostly urban in nature and reflect upon those of the countryside, the larger regional and political entities, and the seas only to the extent that they affected the local urban environment. Forestry, hunting, wildlife, and other related topics are rural rather than urban in character and, accordingly, do not fall within the focus of this book. Since the larger cities such as Venice, Rome, Florence, and Siena tended to be embroiled in broader regional socioeconomic, political, military, and cultural issues involving kings, emperors, and popes, their concerns mirrored those broader issues, frequently to the detriment of their more local and internal interests. As a result, their evidence is introduced only tangentially and as it illustrates the experience of the local units of government.

Finally, we have deliberately sought to place the actions of the urban elites and their statute makers within the context of historical and contemporary reality. Although we do not presume to be able to peer into the exact motivations or imperatives of the elites, we do attempt to provide insight into the cultural, literary, philosophical, and mythical milieu from which they could have sought inspiration and functional models. It is impossible to determine which works or inspirations might have evolved into specific pieces of legislation, but at least it is possible to develop an understanding of the general framework within which the visions that inspired the legislative actions were developed.

In a similar manner, we have attempted to place the environmental accomplishments of the medieval Italian elites within the larger framework of the actions and successes of their classical predecessors. The result is that their successes and achievements are not treated as isolated incidents or historical accidents but rather as the results of deliberate actions by officials acting according to carefully considered rationales. Their actions were not haphazard or accidental: They were rational responses to perceived needs within the limits of the scientific and technological knowledge of the times.

The chapters that follow demonstrate who the early environmentalists were, what ideas and theories motivated them, in what manner they gave shape and form to the environmental programs they devised, and how they carried out and enforced them within the limits of the available technology. The human quest to create a decent world in which to live, to maintain a clean and nurturing environment in which to raise children, and to perpetuate a self-renewing inheritance to pass on to future generations is not merely a newfound goal of twentieth-century environmentalists; rather, it has been the recurring dream of men and women since time immemorial.

1

The Medieval Urban Setting: Politics and Law

The quality of life in the world's cities has long been the concern of urban dwellers, of those who have studied urban issues, and of those who are responsible for the daily decisions that make city life possible. Between the eleventh and eighteenth centuries, the cities of northern and central Italy were in the vanguard of European urban development. Their municipal law codes evolved in direct response to the ever-changing and increasingly demanding needs of an urban population that was growing in size and in political, economic, and social sophistication. Urban residents began to ask for more complex services from city officials, who regulated the various urban industries, crafts, and trades in an effort to provide a safe, sanitary, and healthy environment.

The Medieval Town: Theoretical Foundations

Modern scholarship has created comprehensive models of the preindustrial city. Paul M. Hohenberg and Lynn Hollen Lees, in The Making of Urban Europe, 1000–1950,[1] develop a useful model for the medieval city and its organizational functions. They define the towns as "islands of secular rationality and materialism in medieval society." Following the pioneer work of Max Weber, they look at cities not only as "markets strongly oriented toward the consumption of goods, which they derive from production or trade" but also as "relatively dense settlements having a distinctive economic and political organization."[2] Their sense of community was established upon a relatively free territorial base with distinctive political institutions arising out of a particular combination of fraternal organizations, courts, laws, and at least partial autonomy and self-determination.

According to Hohenberg and Lees, perhaps the most important difference between medieval rural and urban people was their respective political identities. Townspeople, in contrast to their country cousins, were relatively free under the law and had a number of options available to them. Nonetheless, the town—compact, organized, and interdependent—frequently imposed a measure of control over its inhabitants that was more exacting and stringent than villagers could ever imagine. Even if the individual urban citizen had no lord, the town as a corporate entity owed something to a lord, bishop, or king. Fealty was replaced by the concept of association. Townspeople still had ties to the soil, but those ties were reciprocal; they drew profits and sustenance from their landholdings outside of the town, and they expected their town to protect those holdings. The townspeople's relationship to the city was different from that of their rustic cousins. If the townspeople were "of the city," it was *their* city, something that serfs could never say about the manor to which they owed service. But for all of this, the "free air of the town" did not wholly fulfill its promise to the individual.

The medieval town sheltered a "harshly competitive, highly stratified society" that achieved internal peace and order at the cost of systematic repression. Although all adult males in the town were equal in theory, their occupations carried with them significantly different levels of prestige; and the inequities of wealth further widened the gaps between the classes. With time, the power of the elites grew and that of the poor decreased, until the latter became little more than an industrial proletariat with only their labor to sell. Although the smaller towns lacked this precisely defined stratification, there were still clear, if unspoken, distinctions among the wealthy few, the minority of comfortable position, those who normally managed but were essentially propertyless, and a fluctuating fringe of the indigent.[3]

Through intermarriages and alliances of convenience, the most powerful families in Italian towns—merchants, administrators, and nobility—created a patriciate that virtually dominated town councils and communal offices. The frequent inability to maintain peace among themselves led to vicious feuds during the twelfth century. The problem was resolved at least partially in a rather innovative way: An outsider, a neutral party called the podesta, was given magisterial power on a short-term basis and functioned in a manner similar to a modern city manager. In the thirteenth century, the *popolo*,[4] an urban pressure group organized along military lines, appeared to challenge the power of the urban patriciate and its podesta. The social composition of the *popolo* varied from town to town, but the majority of its members were the increasingly powerful guildsmen, who were seeking a measure of control over the destiny of their towns. Although the political control of the town remained firmly in the hands of the elites, the urban workers were also politically active on the basis of kinship ties and personal loyalties. Generally speaking, the loyalties of family, neighborhood, occupation, and clientage tended to override the common interests created by the town's economy.

One of Max Weber's most important contributions to urban history was his conception of the unique "autonomous and autocephalous" nature of the medieval city. Because of the emergence of a newly independent socioeconomic structure in the eleventh and twelfth centuries, which Vatro Murvar defines as the "community or sodality of burghers,"[5] the western European town, including the towns of northern Italy, evolved into a special legal entity with its own administrative council and executive (who was called consul, podesta, or burgomaster). The special character of this legal entity was the separateness (*Scheidung*) of the feudal-peasant and city-burgher spheres. This separateness cannot be found elsewhere in the ancient or oriental city and is unique to the western European town.

Equally unique to the western European urban experience was the tendency of the town elites to continue to increase their own political power, their independence from feudal conventions, and the personal equality of the citizens who resided within the walls of their towns. The assumption of regalian rights and the diminution of the authority of the *extramural* ruler by the local elites was not observed outside of western Europe.[6]

The citizens and ruling elites of the West, unlike the artisan and merchant classes of the ancient and the oriental city, developed a "corporate egalitarian unity based upon religious brotherhood" that effectively prevented the formation of the "magic-animalistic tribal and caste exclusiveness" and "interpersonal connections" so characteristic of the nonwestern city. The Christian community was a religious brotherhood of individual believers who were admitted without regard to kinship, tribal, or similar affiliations. The rights that the individual held in relation to the community and its members were derived from that community (that is, from the brotherhood) and were defined in relation to the other individuals both inside and outside of that community. This exclusiveness is unique to the medieval western European town and is in direct contrast to the conditions in the ancient or oriental city, in which the individual's status was defined in relation to a ruler, tribe, or other kinship group located outside of the walls of the town.

The military and political power of the medieval western town resided within the same brotherhood of citizens. The citizens, as members of the *universita civium* (world of citizens), were required to serve in the town's armed forces at their own expense and, as a result, controlled the local military and political activity. Military power, allegiance, and political clout in the ancient and oriental city, however, were based upon the relationship of the individual to the ruler, a relationship that passed outside of the city limits; under these circumstances, the town was unable to separate itself from the ruler and assert any form of independence because it did not have the means to accomplish this separation.

The western city, unlike its eastern or ancient counterpart, was able to foster conditions that made possible an emergent middle class. This middle class (or *Stand*) was a privileged group, intent on obtaining as many exemptions as possible from the ruler for its own benefit. The eastern merchant, by contrast, dealt directly with the ruler as an individual, and any benefits that derived from the ruler accrued to the merchant personally and not to the class. Medieval Western merchants demanded and obtained concessions from their overlord that enabled them to conduct their business more profitably. The profits thus derived were used to fund the political, military, and economic objectives of the brotherhood of the elite, rather than the projects of the ruler. The freedoms thus acquired by the elites were expanded at every opportunity and were guarded against encroachments by outsiders.

The defense of these freedoms depended upon the interdependence of a number of groups within the town, notably the university, the mendicant and reform-minded religious orders, and the sodalities of university-trained legal experts. These groups were bound together by a number of common interests, if only intermittently, in a world of shifting alliances. One of the stronger threads was the common perception that the town's institutions had to be secularized and maintained as individual units under the control of local elites.

In the medieval western European town, the need to separate the institutions from the religious influences, on one hand, and from the secular power of the ruler, on the other, was imperative. For if the town, its institutions, privileges, and citizens were to remain truly free, then all had to have an existence apart from both ruler and church. Hence, the constant support by the elites for a separate entity was a matter of survival—a survival based on the premise that if the town and its distinctive characteristics were submerged within the greater whole of the church's mysticism or the ruler's authority, it would cease to exist as a distinctive entity.

This struggle was fought out within the context of the law and the legal system. The emerging towns of the eleventh century found common cause with the medieval university in that both saw a need to separate church and secular law. By stressing the concept that canon law, theology, and secular law were distinct entities, the universities and the towns were able to rationalize their respective institutions and initiate the process of separating church and state. Townspeople also supported reform-minded clergy and religious orders that took exception to the financial and political excesses of the regular and secular clergy. However, when the feudal power of churchmen over the medieval town had been effectively broken by the mid-twelfth century, these same townspeople allied themselves and their financial resources with the military and political power of the ruler in an effort to destroy feudal and ecclesiastical resistance.

On the local level, this struggle was reflected in the continuing efforts of the elites to enhance the separation of secular and canon law. This process was advanced by the universities and their graduates, who had been trained in the "logically formed rationality" of Roman procedural law. Canon law, like any other form of sacred law, inevitably attempted to extend its claim of absolute right to rule over all aspects of human behavior. The continuity of this legal and political dualism was maintained by the opposition of the elites and their urban institutions to the encroachments of canon law, especially when their economic interests were threatened by church interference in contracts, usury, and the like. And in the Italian cities, the opposition of the local elites was frequently stiffened by the intervention of the papacy itself, which frequently required the financial and military support of the towns in its struggles with secular powers.

Thus, the interactions of these three distinctive forces produced the unique phenomenon of the medieval Western city, in which all three participated to create a distinctive social organization. Legislation was produced within this urban context to meet local needs. This is not to say that these local statute collections were totally free of outside ecclesiastical or imperial influences, because even the larger towns had to function in an environment in which pope or emperor could (and often did) overwhelm the institutional freedoms of the towns; but these statutes do enshrine in written documents, with increasing frequency and effectiveness over time, local responses designed by local authorities to meet local needs. Unlike the ancient or oriental city in which legislation was made primarily by a central authority that inevitably placed its wider needs before those of local units of government, the legislation produced by the local elites in the medieval western European town was generally representative of local (or regional) interests. The enactment of law codes as an extension of imperial or papal power tended to be the exception rather than the norm. Even towns under the power of larger, stronger neighbors retained enough of the quality of "separateness" to enact legislation representative of their particular internal needs.

The Town Elites

Surrounded as they were by a hostile world, the townspeople and, in particular, the urban elites developed concepts of unity and cooperation as a means of protecting and enhancing their economic, political, and military power. Taking advantage of the anarchy in the Germanic federal system and the deteriorating relationship between the papacy and the imperial government, they began to assert their independence from these traditional authorities during the eleventh century.

In 1035, a powerful class of wealthy leaseholders and minor vassals, encouraged by Emperor Conrad II, staged an abortive revolt against the bishops and the greater feudatories at Milan. Two years later, Conrad issued the *Constitutio de feudis,* which he perceived as yet another means of weakening the ecclesiastical power base. This document extended the right of hereditary succession to subvassals and thereby broke the feudal ties that the bishops and greater lords held over them. Middle-class leaseholders and minor vassals thus became free proprietors bound to Conrad only by the most informal ties.[7]

The town elites pursued policies throughout the eleventh and twelfth centuries that were calculated to pit pope against emperor, thereby keeping townspeople relatively free of feudal obligations and allowing them to pursue their own internal affairs. They minted their own coinage, established tolls and market taxes, regulated weights and measures, and extended their control into the surrounding countryside, or *contado.* Their progress toward urban emancipation, however, was not without conflict.

In spite of a history of almost uninterrupted struggle over the supremacy of church and state, both the papacy and the emperor were committed to the traditional order and their own temporal interests. Indeed, Frederick Barbarossa, upon his accession to the throne in 1156, promised that he would "restore the greatness of the Roman Empire in all of its former power and excellence" and declared that he was dismayed that the governance of the towns of Italy remained in the hands of "young men of inferior rank and ordinary workmen engaged in the lowest mechanical trades."[8]

Although the emperor's outrage at the impudence of townspeople who were willing to challenge the authority of pope and emperor alike may well have been understandable, his characterization of them as the poorer elements of the urban population was inaccurate at best. The ruling elites of the Italian towns were recruited from the towns' richest classes. Whether drawn from noble houses or from those engaged in commerce, industry, crafts, real estate, or administrative services, these people controlled the wealth of the towns in which they resided, and they began to demand a voice in the policymaking activities commensurate with their status and interests.[9]

The direction that a town took to attain its goals was determined by its small, wealthy, ruling elite, whose membership was usually drawn from one or more of the local major occupational categories. Although the exact composition of the ruling elite differed from town to town, the common factor was wealth and the ability to maintain it. These elites had acquired their wealth through control over their town's political and economic life. For example, a town that had developed around the site of a monastery might include a number of wealthy families able to maintain an upper-class lifestyle based on the substantial rents they derived from the same downtown lands that their ancestors had once rented from the monastery for the price of a few eggs or some produce.[10]

To maintain control over their towns, the elites enacted legislation that protected their political and economic positions and enabled them to implement other agendas in their interests. Out of this reality grew the remarkable diversity of the medieval law codes of the northeastern Italian towns.

Constitutional mechanisms varied widely from town to town, as each community sought to develop a legislative system that would meet its particular needs. In the thirteenth century, both the podesta and the *capitano del popolo*[11] worked with elected and appointed governing bodies responsible for the creation of communal law. During this time, the *popolo* often became the dominant party among the many factions within the commune, and the popular council tended to produce legislation of greater importance than that of the podesta.

The councils of the podesta were often more democratic because their membership was rather broadly based and tended to provide for non-*popolo* members. In contrast, the *popolani* (members of the *popolo*), seeking to control the institutions of the commune in their efforts to advance the interests of their class, were opposed to allowing nonelite citizens the opportunity to take control of the legislative bodies and design legislative programs not in accord with the goals of the *popolani*. The situation was reminiscent of that described in George Orwell's *Animal Farm,* in which the revolution to make all animals equal had progressed to the point that although all animals had become equal, some were now *more* equal than others.[12] So it was in most of the towns of northern and central Italy. Although these towns had a number of councils and other bodies associated with the enactment of legislation binding on the commune and its citizens, the most important of these was the *popolo.*[13] As a result, legislation emanating from the councils tended to reflect the interests of the elites rather than those of the general population, although those elites who remained in power for any length of time were astute enough politically to identify with the needs of the general population to the extent necessary to maintain their control.

The Councils

In theory, if not in practice, the most important legislative organ in the thirteenth-century commune was the Greater Council; it was also the one communal institution that maintained the most obvious facade of participatory and democratic involvement by the ordinary citizens of the commune. Having evolved from the Council of the Consuls in the episcopal period, the Greater Council acquired constitutional status as the commune's paramount deliberative and legislative body. Although the number of councillors permitted to serve on the council varied widely from commune to commune there was general uniformity in regard to their qualifications. Council members generally had to meet standards including a minimum age requirement[14] and a minimum standard of conduct, which included such factors as being considered "good men, Catholics and of good reputation, who are not named, excommunicated, or suspected of heresy."[15] Members also had be property owners, taxpayers, and residents. Even though some towns did not permit more than a single member of the same family to serve on the council at any one time, the elites were nevertheless able to dominate these relatively large bodies by using restrictive membership qualifications and controlling the selection process itself.[16] The net result of these elitist policies was a council whose members exhibited the same lineages and whose origins lay within the same socioeconomic stratum. In short, the elites were able to maintain functional control over one of the most effective policymaking bodies of the communal government, and in doing so, they were able to advance the interests of their class and deprive the majority of the commune's citizens of any real or direct control over the destiny of their town.

Matters came to the Greater Council for action or advice from a number of sources. Many issues, such as the regulation of the sale and pricing of bread, the leasing of communal lands, housing specifications, markets, and the maintenance of roads, sewers, and dikes had a statutory basis that required action by the Greater Council. Other agenda items involving diplomacy or special circumstances might be presented on an ad hoc basis, whereas still others were sent there for approval or action by other bodies. Enactments by such organizations as the military companies, guilds, lesser councils, and similar bodies were forwarded for consideration and legislative action. The council, at least during the thirteenth century, had a number of options it could pursue in regard to matters brought to its attention; it could enact or approve, alter, table, flatly reject, or require that provisions be returned to the originating bodies for reconsideration or revision.

Special-interest legislation, stemming from petitions for the redress of grievances, legislative action, or special privileges presented by other bodies, was considered by the Greater Council and usually resulted either in private laws or in legislation affecting the city population as a whole. For example, a citizen whose horse was lost in a military operation authorized by the commune could present a bill for reimbursement to the Lesser Council, which would endorse the claim and forward it to the Greater Council for implementation in the form of a private bill. A council acting on the complaint of a local neighborhood committee that the water from a communal fountain was being fouled by industrial pollutants or the washing of clothes might enact legislation binding upon the entire commune.[17]

Once a matter was presented to the council for action, what transpired? Very few records of the actual deliberations of the councils remain and much of what does is in the form of summaries prepared by notaries[18] employed by the councils. Even these summaries are somewhat suspect because what was recorded is heavily dependent upon the notary who actually made the written copy of the records and upon what those who actually participated in the deliberations wanted revealed.

When a matter was presented for the council's consideration, debate was limited to a fixed number of speakers. When a matter proposed was contrary to an existing statute, the *maggior sindaco,* or judge, made an obligatory *pro forma* statement indicating to the councillors precisely what impact the proposed changes would have on existing law. The council might then act immediately to approve or disapprove the measure at hand. But the council frequently delegated its policymaking or legislative authority to other bodies, most notably to the Lesser Council or special ad hoc legislative bodies. Even when the council acted favorably upon a measure, it would request that another body (again, usually the Lesser Council) actually implement the operation of a particular statute. On other occasions, the Greater Council would create special commissions charged with investigating a particular problem and providing a recommended course of action or a statute upon which the Council of the Whole would act.[19]

The Greater Council could vote on matters before it either openly (by sitting or standing) or by secret ballot. By the onset of the fourteenth century, the open vote had largely been supplanted by the secret ballot. The reason for this was quite obvious, namely, the fear that some councillors would be intimidated by their wealthier, more powerful colleagues.[20]

The actual votes were recorded in a number of ways. In Siena until 1339, councillors were each issued a leaden ball that they dropped into a white or black box to signify affirmative or negative votes. This practice, however, was not particularly secret and the commune adopted the Florentine practice of depositing white or black beans into an urn. This was apparently the common practice in many Italian communes.[21] Although it is not possible to determine whether this procedure was a deliberate attempt by the elites to extend the franchise to additional members of the commune or merely a public relations gesture, it is nonetheless quite evident that the elites controlled the key institutions of the commune by selecting those who would serve on the more compact bodies that chose both the councillors and the topics to be considered by the Greater Council.

By the opening decades of the fourteenth century, the elites realized that in view of increasing urban populations, business activity, and political sophistication of the citizenry, the Greater Councils were no longer the most efficient vehicle whereby they could exercise control over the commune and its institutions. Although the Greater Council was the agency through which the elites obtained the broad base of citizen participation and the commune's official stamp of approval for actions initiated by them, its functional importance began to decline. This decline can be traced in several ways. The records of council deliberations and the lists of those attending council meetings and serving on council commissions become less copious, less informative, and less reliable. Attendance at the session of the Greater Council appears to have begun to decline and the enforcement of the council attendance laws becomes increasingly lax. This clear diminution of the Greater Council's importance could not have occurred without the knowledge and connivance of the elites.[22]

Lauro Marines has pointed out that "small, powerful councils gradually became the most enduring and characteristic institution of the republican system of oligarchy. . . . By 1200, small, short-term councils had become the commune's basic means of rule."[23] Statutes were used to define this system and to spell out the qualifications for officeholding; this was the key to the elites' continuing control of the government. The emphasis that the elites placed on the constitutional and statutory controls over the qualifications, terms, and responsibilities for communal offices can be seen in the various statute collections and in the precision with which they are drawn up.

These smaller, or Lesser, councils were characterized by membership that was constantly changing, since councillors served terms lasting two, six, or twelve months. This afforded many of the elites frequent opportunities to serve in these offices and exercise power; but these opportunities were not endless. Limits on the ability of individuals to succeed themselves in the same offices were designed to enhance the sharing of power among a broader range of elite citizens and to insure that control of the commune would not fall into the hands of a particular party or faction.[24]

The real power in the commune, however, resided in the Lesser, or Ruling, Council.[25] Examples of this type of council included the Nine Governors and Defenders of the People and City of Siena, the Decem Baliae (War Council) and Eight on Security at Florence, and the Council of Ten at Venice. Each commune had a relatively small class of politically active citizens who were deemed to have the qualifications for service on the highest councils. And these men, the richest, the best connected, and the most "experienced," were able to serve on the ruling councils on a more or less continuing basis because they controlled the access to power. Men were "democratically" chosen to serve from "select lists" created by a "scrutiny" or "screening process," usually every three, four, or five years. An ad hoc selection committee, which included "suitable" or "good" men drawn from the guilds, neighborhood groups, or favored political factions, insured the appearance of a democratic process. However, the elites controlled the drawing up of the roster of names from which the "select" list was chosen. Names were then selected from the roster through some random process that tended to produce what Martines defined as a "narrow two-tier ruling caste." At Florence during the pre-Medicean oligarchy, Martines identified an inner circle of some 80–120 individuals who regularly appeared in public office and an outer circle of some 350–450 men who seldom appeared in public office.[26] Within the ruling councils, the facade of democracy remained intact, as most measures required a two-thirds vote before they were implemented. Still, it is quite evident that the ruling urban oligarchy was able to bring its agenda before the Greater Council and keep divisive issues off the floor. Anyone, even a member of the elite, who dared to propose controversial issues before the Greater Council was simply excluded from further participation on the ruling council and thereby denied any effective voice in communal affairs. For those who obeyed the rules, constant service on the ruling councils was the reward.

A Case Study: Bologna 1288

The introduction to the Bologna Statutes of 1288 provides an interesting case history of the manner in which a statute collection might have been created. In April 1287, Jacob Revola, the captain of the Bolognese *popolo*, issued orders that the council and the *popolo* be called together by the traditional ringing of the bell and the call of the town crier. His purpose was to act upon a complaint raised by the town's notaries, who stated that the city's statute collections were very disorganized and useless. Revola then asked the council of the *popolo* to advise him regarding the formation of an ad hoc committee to revise the law code.

The council instructed him to select "certain officials, who were at least thirty years of age and whose number would include two legal experts and four good and well-chosen men who were renowned and well thought of notaries" and to employ them in a manner acceptable to the council and the *popolo* to rectify the problems in the city's statutes. The committee would then be instructed to reduce the mass of conflicting statutes to a "single useful volume." Once the work was complete, the captain of the *popolo* would be required to have all citizens and their households swear to observe the newly published law code and to see to it that four copies of the code were made. The first of these was to be retained by the captain, the second would be deposited in the communal archives, the third would be kept on the desk of the captain (presumably to provide for access by the public), and the fourth was to be placed on the desk of the *bannutires*.[27] The members of the ad hoc committee as well as their households would be guaranteed protection against any reprisals arising out of their work, although they were also warned that their efforts should "not be prejudicial to the lords presently in power or to their households."

The *popolo* met and passed the enabling legislation with a vote of 292–24. The wording of this legislation indicated that the appointees should "be chosen from each quarter of the City of Bologna." The members of the council of the *popolo* were obviously willing to provide for the appearance of a more democratic procedure while maintaining tight control over the selection of those authorized to work on the revision of the statutes. Communal officials were instructed to provide a sufficient salary for the appointees and "a place where they could stay" while working on the project. The current and succeeding podestas were required to compel communal officials to carry out their responsibilities "in accordance with the form of the aforesaid provision."

However, this well-defined process somehow broke down. On July 21, 1288, nearly fourteen months after the effective date of the enabling legislation and a year after the selection of the ad hoc commission, the new captain of the *popolo*, the noble Lord Bressanus de Sala, summoned the *popolo* to meet in council in the new palazzo of the commune. He proposed that the work of the ad hoc commission be continued under the terms of the previous legislation, with the additional stipulations that the work be completed by October 1288, that salaries would not be paid to the commissioners after that date, and that the captain would have the authority to compel them to complete the work under detention if necessary. The new legislation was voted on by a secret ballot with the use of white and black beans and was passed by a vote of 264–56. The threat to withhold salaries and to confine the commissioners was effective; the newly revised statutes were presented to the council of the *popolo* on October 1, 1288.[28]

Considering the fact that the previous revision had taken place in 1267, the revision of 1288 was sorely needed. The quality of the ad hoc commission's work was so noteworthy (in spite of that body's procrastination) that the 1288 edition of the Bologna statutes remained in effect until 1318, when profound political changes required another revision.

This process is especially interesting because it provides clear insight into the workings of a commune as it created a new law code, and it is also illustrative of the manner in which the oligarchy exercised its control over the daily functions of the town and its people. Bologna, in 1287–1288, was a town noted for neither its political stability nor for harmonious relations among its numerous factions. Yet the elites acting through the *popolo* controlled the revision of the fundamental law code regulating the daily activities of the Bolognese citizenry by selecting the individuals who rewrote the law code. The democratic niceties—the secret ballots, the surveillance of the "scrutiny" by neutral churchmen, and so on—were carefully observed, but the elites suffered no loss of power or prestige, and the town population apparently accepted the process without any documented disturbances.

Once the law was duly enacted and published, it became binding upon the members of the commune. Enforcement of the law and, in general, the effectiveness of communal institutions depended heavily not only upon the consent and the goodwill of the governed but also upon the capability and willingness of the commune to maintain peace within the city walls and to insure that its laws and regulations were being observed.

Perhaps the last real check on the power of the elites was the power of the courts to interpret and administer the commune's law. Communal officials realized that there was no point in making law unless there was a firm determination to enforce that law.[29] To enforce the law, a multiplicity of courts was created, including those of the podesta, the captain of the *popolo,* and the merchant guilds; each of these institutions felt that its unique interests could best be protected if it had a court staffed with personnel loyal to its interests that would deal with those matters falling under its particular jurisdiction. Although these were generally courts of final resort, constitutional guidelines could be circumvented when the need arose. Cases involving conspiracy, treason, rebellion, and special petitions could induce communal officials to abrogate normal court jurisdictions and constitutional guarantees. For example, the Siena Greater Council took a case involving treason out of the podestal court in 1314 and remanded it to the Court of the Nine.[30] The ruling council had also enacted ad hoc legislation on October 15, 1311, which allowed the podesta to ignore constitutional safeguards regarding the use of torture during interrogation in conspiracy cases.[31]

Under normal circumstances, the various courts were staffed by the principal magistrates or by lesser administrative officers. It was not abnormal for the same magistrate to conduct an investigation, apprehend the culprit, and then try the case and sentence the individual. Although there is little published documentation extant to provide an in-depth study of the daily operations of these courts, it is evident from the statute collections that the communes frequently experimented with their court systems in an effort to better manage their day-to-day operations and more effectively define the jurisdiction and authority of the communal courts themselves.

In sum, the elites controlled the entire process of lawmaking, law enforcement, and the interpretation of the law itself. This afforded the elites real power in the commune—a power whose exercise was low profile and even had some semblance of democracy, but which was all-pervasive and well suited to the control of the majority of the people in the town by a select and powerful ruling class. The legislation enacted by the elites reflected their interests. Thus, since it is highly unlikely that the desires of the general urban population would be enshrined in the law codes unless the elites concurred, the environmental concerns addressed in the codes were concerns felt by the elites. As such, the law codes serve as an effective focus of study to determine the policies that the elites were willing to enforce under the law in their attempts to provide for a suitable quality of life in their towns.

The members of the elite leadership were therefore compelled to enact legislation that would protect not only their political and economic position within the communities but also the environmental resource base upon which so much of their power rested. Since they wished to bring order and a reasonable quality of life to communities where precedents for doing so were scarce, they looked to the law to provide a functional basis for this reorganization. Municipal officials looked to Roman and canon law and other legal precedents to formulate the legal codes that enabled them to govern their towns and protect their political and economic interests effectively. But where were they to find the vision that anticipated the end result of their efforts to protect the environment and provide for a suitable quality of life for their citizens? Fortunately, the western European secular and religious literary tradition offered the Italian elites the kind of vision that would enable them to ultimately create the fabulous cities of the Italian Renaissance.

2

Ancient and Medieval Environmental Spokesmen

Although it has been fashionable to claim that environmental awareness or even sensitivity to the environment is a recent development, the fact is that the human concern for the environment is thousands of years old. The classical origins occur in the notion that there was unity and harmony in the universe. From this was derived the idea of purpose in creation, the notion that the universe, as we know it, has resulted from the planned, rational, and intelligent actions of a creative entity.

Classical Environmental Theory

Plato (427–347 B.C.E.), writing in the *Timaeus*,[1] advanced the concept of an artisan deity, of a mind imposing itself on "reluctant matter." Deep within Greek thought was the notion of respect for the artisan and for the beauty and order that was produced by the application of intelligence and manual skill to unformed matter. Within this context, the human was thought capable of producing order and beauty in nature and of exercising control over nature through intelligence and skill. The artisan deity in turn saw to it that the world or universe would remain eternal and divine.

Aristotle (384–322 B.C.E.) placed greater reliance upon the power of Nature to order itself to meet the perceived needs of humankind. Aristotle thought that the nature and distribution of plants and animals were ordered to meet human needs and purposes, that is, so ordered to produce food, clothing, shelter, and various implements. Even if the arguments advanced in the *Politica*[2] do not explain all of the purposes in nature (e.g., although the skin may exist to delimit the body, why does it have color?), Aristotle clearly stated that nature exists for human uses. This theme was be taken up again and again by later writers.[3]

Cicero (106–43 B.C.E.), in writing *De natura deorum*[4] and reflecting the Stoicism of Posidonius, advanced the twin notions of the aesthetic beauty and the utility of the earth: The earth is a beautiful place in which the human mind creates the tools, machines, and processes that enable humans to enhance the world's beauty and meet their ever-evolving needs. Pliny (circa 23–79 C.E.), on the one hand, saw humankind as abusing the kind, indulgent, fertile earth[5] but, on the other hand, he argued that humans could take the initiative and maintain the earth through care and husbandry.[6]

Although various Epicurean thinkers sought later on to diminish the role of the artisan deity or the arguments for a divine design based upon their observations of the imperfections of nature, the human impact upon nature was not diminished but was instead given a serious negative connotation.

The Hippocratic treatise entitled "Airs, Waters, Places," a singularly disorganized and fragmented work, introduced a number of misconceptions into Western scientific thought that influenced later medieval writers. The authors established decidedly unscientific relationships between culture and the environment, occupation and disease, and geographic location and human institutions. In the absence of the scientific method, medieval writers made frequent use of the Hippocratic literature to explain human nature in terms of environment and to attempt to convince their readers that people were shaped by their environment, rather than the reverse.

Although the majority of classical and Hellenistic writers perceived a lofty intellectual or philosophical human role in shaping and directing the environment, they were also beginning to realize that people and their industry, agriculture, and crafts played a formative, pragmatic role in the environmental changes that they were observing. Michael Rostovtzeff has supplied ample evidence[7] that Hellenistic Greeks enthusiastically introduced crop and plant innovations, reclaimed land, planted and harvested trees, and developed and fertilized cropland, all with the clear intent and purpose of improving the land and enriching its owners.[8]

Strabo (circa 64 B.C.E.–23 C.E.) writes of the efficiency of Egyptian efforts to impose human control over the Nile River basin:

> The attention and care bestowed upon the Nile is so great as to cause industry to triumph over nature. The ground by nature, and still more by being supplied with water produces a great abundance of fruits. By nature also a greater rise of the river irrigates a larger tract of land; but industry has com-

pletely succeeded in rectifying the deficiency of nature, so that in seasons when the rise of the river has been less than usual, as large a portion of the country is irrigated by means of canals and embankments, as in seasons when the rise of the river has been greater.[9]

Finally, the author of a Hermetical treatise made it clear that humans take an active, purposeful role in the alteration of their environment and, while doing so, fulfill their ordained role in the grand design of God:

And when I say "the things of earth," I do not mean merely the two elements of earth and water, which nature has placed in subjugation to men: I mean all things that men do on land and water, or make out of the earth and water, as for instance tillage and pasture, building, harbour-works and navigation, and intercourse and mutual service, that strong bond by which members of the human race are linked together. [For to man is given the charge] of that part of the universe which consists of earth and water; and this earthly part of the universe is kept in order by means of man's knowledge and application of the arts and sciences. For God willed that the universe should not be complete until man had done his part.[10]

Thus, it is clear that classical and Hellenistic writers, and by extension, their readers, clearly understood that they had been given the "stewardship of a divinely ordered earth"[11] and that through such activities as irrigation, agriculture, plant development, the construction of roads, and the beautification of towns, they were functioning as God's partners in creating the earth's perfection. Nevertheless, it was equally clear that people could and did deny their stewardship role and participated in the destruction of their earthly environment through deforestation, animal overkill, flooding land, and other such activities with negative consequences. Humanity was not a passive spectator but rather had been presented with a clear challenge: Master the environment and fulfill the Divine Plan or defy the work of God and Nature through the willful and capricious abuse and destruction of the environment.

Christian and Medieval Environmental Theory

The historian of medieval civilization is faced with a vast range of writings by Christian authors. In order to find an intellectual underpinning for the legislative activities of a small group of municipal leaders who flourished between the eleventh and fourteenth centuries, it is necessary to narrow the focus of the search for environmental theory to the thoughts of prominent Christian and medieval writers who were concerned with two specific concepts: the earth as a planned abode and humans as the stewards of their environment. The selection of prominent authors is justified by their availability and by the likelihood that their works were read by the elites or their advisers or were expounded upon in sermons, discussions, or similar intellectual exchanges.

Since the beginning of the Judeo-Christian tradition, it was made clear in theoretical writings that humans and the earth on which they live are both creatures of a caring God. The thematic linkage between the two creations is God's continuing care for the world. Just as creation is evidence for the existence of God, so the beauty and utility of creation direct humans to their destiny—life after death.[12] God has granted the human race a divine mission to control all of creation and has endowed humans with the ability and power to carry out that mandate. To accomplish this end, the human race was intended by God to multiply, occupy the earth, and secure his dominion over nature.

God's act of creation in bringing the order of nature to chaos is a *creatio continua*[13] (continual creation), requiring his continuing concern, solicitude, and attention, through human agency. Adam is set down in the Garden of Eden "to till it and keep it."[14] The Fall of Man becomes an important Christian theme because the disorder and decay observed within nature are traceable to deliberate human actions rather than as pagan authors posited, to any natural organic aging process within the world itself.

Nevertheless, in spite of being disobedient people are given the earth as their habitation[15] and are expected to exercise their dominion over it as controller and modifier of the earthly environment. This domination is at least partially manifested through the human domestication of animals and the power to take animal life in order for people to provide themselves with food, clothing, and shelter.[16] The human function is to carry out the Divine Plan of the Creator, walking "beside him, like a master workman."[17]

The relationships among God, humanity, and the earth are not as clearly defined in the New Testament. Although Paul expressed the concern that people lose sight of the Creator amid the works of creation,[18] he did express his conviction that humans retain a significant role in the Divine Plan: "For we are fellow workmen for God; you are God's field, God's building."[19] And furthermore: "Everything created by God is good and nothing is to be rejected, if it is received with thanks given."[20]

In Romans 1:20, Paul stated, "Ever since the creation of the world, his invisible nature, namely his eternal power and duty have been clearly perceived in the things that have been made." The argument in Romans 1:20 became a strong bulwark against later writers who were tempted to reject the earth as the fit dwelling place for man and to express hatred for nature. Paul, however, adopted a *theologia naturalis* (theology of nature) in which creation is viewed as the work of a kind, loving, and reasonable creator.

In Romans 8:18–39, Paul clearly argued that all of creation "waits with eager longing for the revealing of the sons of God."[21] Creation and humankind, he claimed, are striving for the perfection that is in God, and because of God's indwelling spirit, they are doing so in hope. Perhaps this is the most important support that Christians are given in the New Testament. In spite of the consequences of the Fall, humanity has been given the hope of salvation and the belief not only that the imperfection of the world is a part of God's plan but that the perfection of creation will be accomplished within the Divine Plan, with the assistance and cooperation of humans.

The Earth as a Planned Abode

The classical concept of the earth as a planned abode passed easily into the writings of Christian authors. Among the earliest was Origen (circa 185 C.E.–circa 254 C.E.), who, in his work entitled *Contra Celsum*, argued that God intentionally provided a home for humankind because he favored the rational over the irrational.[22] God created the human as a rational being, thus human needs were greater than those of irrational beings. Because of the urgency of these needs, humans were compelled to use their minds and discover the arts, whereby, as God's helpers on the earth, people would complete and improve creation. Similarly, through the use of intelligence, humans were able to tame and domesticate wild animals and convert them to their uses. The presence of domesticated animals was proof both of the rational superiority of humans and of their consequent cooperation in the Divine Plan.

> The Creator, then, has made everything to serve the rational being and his natural intelligence. For example, we use animals for such functions as guarding flocks or herds of cattle or goats or for carrying burdens or baggage. Similarly lions, bears, leopards, boars, and animals of this sort, are said to have been given to us in order to develop the seeds of courage in us.[23]

Augustine (354–430 C.E.), writing in *The City of God,* penned a stinging rebuke to Origen's lack of understanding of the rationale for the creation expressed in Genesis 1:31 ("And God saw everything that He had made, and behold it was very good.")[24] Augustine pointed out that God created a world of order out of his goodness and because of his pleasure in creating.[25] The world was therefore not created for man or for his rationality; God created the world to serve his purposes alone. Thus, if people domesticated animals or brought order to untamed land, it was done at God's will, although humans retained the free will to choose to ignore that which the divine plan clearly mandated.

Augustine also clearly distinguished between order in nature and human evaluations of it. He cautioned that one must never forget that both nature and earth are creations of God and that although God's creations may be characterized by beauty, man should not lose himself in that beauty, thereby forgetting their Creator and the City of God. Even within the context of his preoccupation with the City of God, Augustine was able to see men and women, as creatures of God, as both being assisted by God and as assisting God in the completion of creation. Humans have been able to utilize their God-given intelligence and skill to create the arts that have made possible their societies and cultures. Those skills and arts, when directed to fulfill the plan of the "Supreme and Unchangeable God, emphasize man's proper role, namely that of seeking the City of God."[26]

There was support for the concept of the earth as a planned abode from a source contemporaneous with Christ. Philo the Jew (circa 20 B.C.E.–circa 45 C.E.) asserted human dominance over, and responsibility for, the environment with these words: "So the Creator made man all things, as a sort of driver and pilot, to drive and steer things on earth, and charged him with the care of animals and plants."[27]

The early medieval Christian view of the earth represented an amalgamation of several schools of thought deriving from Plato, the Neoplatonists, and finally, Augustine. Within this context, the earth represented the finished product of the Divine Artisan, and there was a natural order in which all things had a place according to the Divine Plan. Even the human had a purpose—to assist in the completion of the Artisan's work through the ordering of nature. And, lest humans lose sight of their secondary role in the process of creation, Augustine unceremoniously reminded them that they were creatures of God, no less than the world itself, and that, although their attention was fixed on the perfection of the earth according to God's will, their proper task was to keep the mind and soul firmly fixed on the City of God.

Albert the Great (circa 1200–1280), the teacher of St. Thomas Aquinas, posited a natural theology that was based on learning and observing. He believed that to the extent that human knowledge was incomplete, the knowledge of God and his designs had to remain incomplete. Albert consistently emphasized the concept of a divinely designed earth within the framework of the Aristotelian philosophy of nature. He recognized that human endeavor played an active role in environmental change. Through his travels, he observed and commented upon the effects on plants of manuring, tilling the soil, seeding, and he discussed the pruning and grafting of trees, the cultivation of fields, meadows, vineyards, and orchards, and the deleterious effects of deforestation and erosion.[28]

St. Thomas Aquinas (c. 1224–1274) viewed creation in a more abstract form and utilized its order, utility, beauty, and harmony to explain the existence of God. In his *Summa Contra Gentiles,*[29] he advanced a rigorous natural theology in which the Aristotelian concepts of order, planning, and design were linked to an emphasis on the beauty of creation reminiscent of his mentor, Albert. Nature, he maintained, is essentially good. The universe is an organic whole in which each constituent part exists to serve its particular purpose. Nature, contrary to the belief expressed earlier by Origen, is not an outcome of sin; rather, the entire universe is a creation of God reflecting his glory and goodness.[30]

He further argued that the beauty we observe in creation is a function of the divine creative act.[31] Aquinas's description of the beauty of Paradise provides an insight into what he considered a desirable physical environment, namely, a place with a temperate climate, probably located in a region in the eastern quadrant of the world, peopled by workers busy perfecting God's creation.[32] The place of humanity in the hierarchy of being,[33] somewhere between the angels and the animals, is perfectly consistent with the power to use plants and animals for personal benefit and to shape the environment to meet human needs.[34]

Although Aquinas's ideas do not differ significantly from the ideas expressed by earlier writers, they do provide an intellectual basis for his contemporaries to control and shape the environment around them. The human race, functioning in a hierarchy of being, rules those entities below it and adopts benign Nature to its multiple purposes by virtue of the rationality and the divine spark placed in it by God. Thus, humanity's actions in exercising power over the environment should be tempered by humility and wisdom.

Aquinas, unlike many of his predecessors, had an opportunity to apply his theoretical knowledge to a practical situation. In his work entitled *On Kingship: To the King of Cyprus,* he brought together relevant portions of the Aristotelian corpus (notably, the *Politics* and the *Physics*), and works by

Vitruvius and Vegetius[35] in an effort to remind earthly rulers (in this case, possibly Hugh II of Cyprus, whose royal house had maintained friendly ties with the Dominicans) that they should model their rule upon the example of God's creation of the world. The ruler, he counseled, should "first choose a suitable place which will preserve the inhabitants by its healthfulness, provide the necessities of life by its fruitfulness, please them with its beauty, and render them safe from their enemies by its natural protection."[36] Thus, the ruler is accorded a role in creation, although on a plane much lower than that of God.

Implementing the Aristotelian Golden Mean, Aquinas advised the ruler to seek out a temperate climate since the inhabitants would benefit from longer, healthier lives,[37] the military security of the town would be enhanced by an improved ability to wage war and train soldiers,[38] and the political life of the citizens would flourish because of the salubrious effects of the climate.[39]

Calling upon classical authorities, Aquinas insisted that the site of a city should have good air and good water. The degree of healthiness could be determined by the condition of the food and animals produced in a given place, and the appearance of the people themselves would provide a good indication of the healthiness of a site.[40] The best site would be self-sufficient in terms of food and water, although ease in obtaining food through trade would be considered a compensating factor. Unfortunately, trade and commerce with foreigners, he noted, could cause harm to the town's civic customs: "Foreigners with their different customs cannot be expected to act like citizens, who, however, may be led from their own ways by the examples of strangers."[41] Trade in itself often led to excess because it fostered greed, tended to weaken the effectiveness of the military, and concentrated the population within the confining walls of the town, which in turn led to dissension and sedition. Trade, like so many other things, was necessary, but it had to be practiced with moderation.

Finally, he thought the beauty of the town's site—its broad meadows, rolling hills, lush forests, lakes, and waters—must engender a sense of loyalty and affection in the hearts of its inhabitants, although the site must not be immoderately beautiful, lest the judgment of the senses be dulled by too much pleasure.

The importance of Aquinas's essay on kingship lies in its comparison of kingly rule on earth with the divine rule of the universe. Although it is little more than a thirteenth-century recapitulation and distillation of classical ideas on the relationship between the physical environment and health and on the role of moderation in governance and civil society, the emphasis upon the role of reason in governance and the creation of a kingdom is novel. The king, as a being of reason and intelligence, should, like God as the creator of the universe, plan the creation of towns and kingdoms with care and deliberation and should act only after considering the air, water, and land quality before dedicating resources to the task.

Stewardship in Action

After laying out the broad, if not all-inclusive, outlines of an intellectual framework for the concept of environmental awareness in medieval Europe, we may proceed to the next task, namely, determining whether this concept had any practical impact in the real world, on the everyday activities of the men and women who lived in the world that the theorists so copiously wrote about. There is little doubt that the popular culture—the commonly held beliefs of ordinary men and women—had a daily and pragmatic influence upon the decisions of the political leadership; however, the evidence of the environmental statutes suggests that medieval leaders were seeking intellectual models that would empower them to rise above the legacy of the past—the legacy of deforested countrysides, polluted water, and smog-shrouded cities. The practical needs of the industrialist, the butcher, and the craftsman had to be balanced against the aesthetic demands of the intellectual models implicit in the literature available to the medieval leadership. To develop an understanding of how municipal leaders accomplished this balance, it is necessary to narrow the focus of this investigation to a manageable level and, for this purpose, the medieval concept of stewardship in action will be limited to medieval municipal waste management and the local governmental attempts to limit municipal pollution.

Recent scholarship has demonstrated that medieval people were driven to create an environment as clean and healthy as their technology, priorities, and civilization permitted. Medieval Italians were environmentally conscious and undertook strong efforts to protect their environment. This is underscored by one of the era's strongest critics, Georgius Agricola (George Bauer, 1494–1555). In a passage decrying the negative effects of mining operations on the environment, he stated that medieval Italians were warned by law that

> no one should dig the earth for metals and so injure their very fertile fields, their vineyards, and their olive groves. Also they argue that the woods and the groves are cut down, for there is a need for an endless amount of wood

for timbers, machines, and the smelting of metals. And, when the woods and groves are felled, then are exterminated the beasts and the birds, very many of which furnish a pleasant and agreeable food for man. Further, when the ores are washed, and the water which has been used poisons the brooks and streams, and either destroys the fish or drives them away. Therefore, the inhabitants of these regions, on account of the devastation of their fields, woods, groves, brooks and rivers, find great difficulty in procuring the necessities of life, and by reason of the destruction of the timber they are forced to greater expense on erecting buildings.[42]

This statement is important for two reasons. First, medieval Italians clearly understood that industrial production produced a significant impact upon the environment. Second, the law was used to regulate industrial activities to protect the community's environment, resource base, and quality of life.

Because of the nature of the science and technology of the era, the medieval conception of pollution was far more subjective than equivalent modern descriptions. For example, in modern times, federal, state, and municipal legislation regulating odors emanating from tanneries and butcher shops enforces measurable tolerance levels far more severe than those that would be expected of a society lacking adequate refrigeration and containment technologies. Indeed, some of the medical lore of the medieval era indicated that the confined air of the town was more healthful that the open air of the fields and forests.

Medieval Italian water and land pollution standards tend to reflect modern norms because the effects of pollutants were perceptible to the regulators and had an immediate impact upon the physical and financial well-being of the town's citizens. Discoloration and bad taste in the water were more clearly understood concepts: Polluted water made people sick, and dirty water reduced the quality of products employing water in their manufacture. Land rendered unusable or simply less useful because of industrial or agricultural pollutants adversely affected a town's economic survival. As a result, local standards were established to maintain levels of water and land quality that were tolerable and measurable within the context of medieval science and technology.

Trade-related environmental legislation tended to reflect the diversity of interests among the power brokers of the communes. Although there were few tradesmen and artisans serving on the policymaking bodies initially, their numbers and representation increased as their wealth and economic power developed. Already organized by occupation and common interests into guilds, tradesmen gravitated toward political organizations like the *societas popoli*, a more formal name for the *popolo*. The *popolo* served as a pressure group designed to counterbalance the social weight of the powerful and the lawless and to achieve for its members a considerable constitutional role in the commune. Legislation arising out of this political arena reflected the diversity of the town's political and socioeconomic experience and because such legislation was developed within the "give and take" of the political arena, it reflected needs imperative enough to require the cooperation of diverse, competing elements of the commune.

In more specific situations, laws were enacted to control the economic behavior of various classes of tradesmen. For example, the butcher guilds were regulated to insure the maximum production of the foodstuffs required by the local population at the lowest possible prices and with the least significant impact upon the communal environment. One approach employed by the local elites to limit pollution within the city was the restriction of the number of places where butcher shops might be located. For example, Ferrara's statute makers told their butchers that people who pay taxes "could freely build a butcher shop on whatever portion of the bank of the Po they wished from the headland of the bank of the Po all the way to the other headland in the city and anywhere on the bank."[43]

Limiting the number of butcher shops had the practical effect of reducing the volume of the waste products dumped within the town's environment. Butcher shops in each town slaughtered and sold thousands of animals annually; the inevitable result of this activity was thousands of pounds of blood, entrails, and other waste products. There was a conscious effort to require butchers and meat sellers to practice their trade in a manner that would not be injurious to the health of the city's inhabitants and that would leave the city's roads and waterways free of animal by-products.

There was an additional reason for locating the butcher shops in specific areas and quarters of the city. A common problem was the disposal of animal wastes. In Bologna, Bassano, and Verona, the butchers dumped the waste into the streets until the city fathers banned the practice; then, they dumped the waste products into vacant fields until that practice was also banned and the butchers were explicitly told to take the waste products out of the city.[44]

Ferrara, like many other cities, solved the problem by locating its butcher shops along waterways and "decreeing that butchers should have one ditch or cesspool next to their butcher shops, into which the blood of animals should be thrown, and that this pit or cesspool should be enclosed so that pigs and other animals should not have their way and fall into that ditch."[45]

The medical lore of the age and common sense told the statute makers that the waste problem had to be dealt with, but their technology did not provide adequate answers. The primary solutions available to them were containment or disposal into a moving body of water downstream from local drinking-water sources.

The economic success of the leather workers' guilds was loosely tied to the success of the butchers. The difficulty facing the medieval commune in regard to tanners was that the tanning process itself created serious pollution within the town's walls. The tanning process was complex and required the use of toxic chemicals, including such exotic solutions as slaked lime, a chicken-, pigeon-, and dog-dung mixture, tannic acid, and a mildly acidic concoction derived from fermenting bran. Once cleaned, leather was prepared for production through one of several chemical-based processes designed to preserve the leather and prevent decay.[46]

The two-phase tanning process was conducted first in open pits and then continued in vats. The process was slow, but thorough, requiring some fifteen months before hides were completely tanned. The process obviously produced a large amount of chemical wastes that found their way into the commune's waterways and sewer systems. One of the primary concerns of the statute makers was to prevent this sort of environmental abuse.

The Ferrarese statute makers, almost as an afterthought, appended a statute to the end of the Fourth Book of the Code of 1287. The statute simply states "that no leather worker or any other person can nor should in any way or at any time remove the flesh or hair [from any hide] or intestines next to the cesspool of the City of Ferrara nor next to the Po on the side of the city."[47]

The restrictions in Bassano were more explicit. Leather workers were warned that they could not "strip the flesh from hides, wash hides, or place any waste in the streets or in the waters from the Bridge of the Brenta downstream to the end of the structure near the water on the bank of the Campus Marcius." The animal wastes "should be dragged onto the Campus Marcius and down into the ditch in the middle and nowhere else."[48] This law was far more specific than the Bassano law of 1259, which simply stated that no one should "strip the flesh from the hides or place the hides in or next to the Brenta River." Bassanese tanners were also warned to practice their trade without creating nuisances by storing hides in or around butcher shops or by greasing the hides in the streets, porticos, or meadows of the town.[49] Again, there is a definite effort to restrict the area in which the tanners could practice their trade and dispose of their waste products, but no attempt was made to restrict the practice of the trade itself.

Verona, also concerned about water quality, insisted its leather workers not work or soak leather or hides "in the River Fossatum."[50] The next statute in the Veronese code is a curious mixture of concerns. The law begins thus: "No one should throw or cause anything to be thrown into the River Adige, or into its streams, narrows, banks, or into any sewers during the day."[51] It goes on to specify other locations and to ban the disposal of clearly defined industrial and craft-related waste products in the water ways of the commune.[52] Then, the statute makers relent and state, "But, during the night only, is it permitted to throw this material into running water only."[53] Tanners, their apprentices, and equipment were also banned from the streets near the palace of the commune.

The products of the leather industry were necessary to the commune; the unfortunate by-product of this necessity was chemical and organic pollution, not to speak of the smells attendant upon a tannery's operation. Accordingly, the tanneries themselves appear to have been kept away from the political and commercial hubs of the town whenever possible and their waste products removed from the city at places and times that would not cause problems with the town's drinking water.

An important source of protein in the medieval diet was fish and other marine products. These foods had to be cleaned, dried, or salted, and their processing was also regulated by the communal governments. Bassano, Ferrara, and Verona were all inland cities located on rivers that apparently had fish populations substantial enough to support a fish market and related industrial operations. The Veronese concern regarding the supply of fish and its sale within the city was typical of riverine towns. The supply was limited and intended solely for the local markets.[54] To maintain a constant supply of fish, legislation was enacted mandating that fishnets were to have meshes "two fingers" wide, multihooked lines were not to be used, and no one was permitted to fish throughout the month of February.[55] And these rules were to be enforced by communal guards.[56] Concern for the safety and health of the commune's citizens is embodied in statutes enjoining fishermen from dirtying the marketplace and from polluting the riverbank with fish intestines and other waste.[57]

The commune of Piran, located on the Adriatic Coast, had slightly different concerns. Like the inland cities, Piran insisted that fish caught in its marshes and waters be sold in the communal markets.[58] Piran, however, exercised more comprehensive control over its fishermen and fisheries. Fishermen were required every April to report to the Communal Palace[59] to elect stewards from their number who would swear to faithfully represent their interests to the podesta.[60] The fisheries themselves were staked each year from the first of May until the end of August by the podesta and stewards;[61] the purpose of staking the fisheries was to control access to them during the fishing season[62] or when the fisheries were sealed and to fine those who broke the law.[63] With carefully defined exceptions, the fisheries were not to be fished with dragnets. Access to them was to be controlled from September to March.[64] All fish that were caught were to be preserved and presented to the stewards, presumably to be taxed and sold in the marketplace.[65] The Piranese statute makers did not want pollution to sully the town's shores and waters, and they acted to prevent the disposal of waste materials into communal waters. They also denied a license for the construction of a fish-oil press where it could pollute the fisheries.[66]

The clear intent of the fishery-related legislation was similar to that regulating butchers, namely, to insure an adequate food supply in a manner that protected communal health, safety, and local water resources.

Clothiers, flax workers, and cloth makers of almost every stripe come under the scrutiny of the commune as well. The flax-retting process[67] was the most serious concern of the statute makers. Medieval cloth manufacturers developed many variations of the retting process in order to utilize different water supplies, including ditches, sewers, streams, and fountains. When they used the commune's drinking water or sewers, they came into conflict with the communal authorities.[68]

During the cleaning process, soap, stale urine, lye-water, various alkaline detergents, fuller's earth, and sulfur were commonly used and frequently found their way into the communal waterways. Bassano and Verona enacted legislation enjoining the cloth guilds from washing wool and wool fell or from soaking flax in the town's waterways. The guilds were also warned against storing unprocessed flax, ashes, old wood, or other chemicals within the town. Ferrara simply forbade them to prepare flax within its jurisdiction and allowed them to keep only enough flax for family use; sales of flax were specifically forbidden under penalties of fines and confiscation. Once again, communal authorities recognized a causal relationship between the by-products of cloth production and the pollution of the town's water resources, and they acted to limit the impact of that pollution.

Thus, the communes did express some very definite environmental concerns through their legislation. The supply of food and water was a primary concern of the communes. They sought to protect that supply through legislation forbidding guilds to engage in practices that would pollute the communal environment. Conservation practices were exhibited in enhanced communal control over food and land resources, in attempts to control the equitable distribution of food and water supplies, and in attempts to prevent hoarding or unfair and unequal trade practices.

Does this reflect anything other than economic or political self-interest? Within the limited context of the examples provided here, the answer is yes. The theoretical literature insists that humans serve as the stewards of this world. Stewardship implies, at the very least, the management and protection of the resources at one's command. The protection of the municipal water resources from the polluting effects of industrial processes (notably, the effects of the slaughtering of animals, the preparation of fish, and the processing of cloth and leather) through the imposition of restrictive legislation demonstrates not only an awareness of the problem but the willingness to take effective action to accomplish the goal. Whether or not the town elites were seeking divine approval for being "God's partner in the full development of the earthly Eden" and for employing "practical knowledge of the powers of nature" to complete the earth is an open question; that they did find a compelling reason to do so is not. A thorough reading of the statutes of town councils and any other extant records would certainly yield deeper insight into their motivation.

The case of Book 10 of the Piranese statute collection of 1307 presents an even stronger case for positive conscious action on the part of a town council to exercise stewardship over a natural resource. Unlike its riverine sister towns, which were largely content to manage the pollution associated with fisheries and fish markets, Piran undertook to exercise comprehensive control over its fishery. The fish themselves were seen as a resource to be preserved. The town may have acted out of self-interest, but in any case, the extent of the Piranese legislation is unique. The Piranese elites sought to control who fished, when they fished, where they fished, and how they fished. The catch itself was monitored by knowledgeable officials and by the fishermen themselves. Was this done solely for the purposes of taxation? Possibly, but not likely. Finally, there is the problem of the tenth statute in Book 10. A local business, a factory that was producing fish oil from the locally caught product, was required by statute to relocate lest it pollute the waters of the fishery with its waste products. Could this be perceived as a purely business decision? Again, possibly, but not likely. It would have been cheaper for the businessman, who probably was one of the elites and who certainly employed townspeople, to have remained where he was. Thus, it would appear that this is a clear example of a town government acting as the steward of its resources to preserve its resources for reasons that go beyond those of mere economics.

The Vision of an Urban Utopia

There is clear evidence that by the High Middle Ages, a model of the ideal city was beginning to emerge from the writings of a wide range of philosophers, prophets, scholastics, and scholars stretching back to the earliest of the Greek writers. Literary evidence found in the writings of scholars in the tenth through the fourteenth centuries suggests that the concept was of interest to them and of sufficient interest to their communities to remain an increasingly compelling subject of their debates.

Just what was the ideal city and what did it look like? It certainly was not Augustine's City of God, nor was it the bejeweled, flaming visions of Enoch and the Apocalypse, the fanciful Jerusalem of the Bible and the Hereford map, the fabled Babylon, or the magnificent Rome of the Caesars. Nor was it a city like Marco Polo's Cathay or one of the towering, turreted cities of the crusaders' Middle East. Yet, perhaps, it was a bit of all of them.

Certain descriptive trends were beginning to emerge from the scholarly and fanciful literature of the day. Possibly, the most dominant feature of the emerging ideal city was its beauty. This city was adorned with the finest stone, decorated with the best jewels. Fire, bright colors, and brilliance all added their allure to the description. Aristotle and Albert the Great each added the dimension of the idyllic settings into which these towns were placed—areas characterized by flowing waters, lush forests, fertile fields, and temperate climates.

The city was also to be the epitome of order. Government would be hierarchical, and its kings, cast in the mold of Aquinas's King of Cyprus, Aristotle's model of temperance, and the biblical type, the just king, would rule benignly in imitation of the Creator, leading the people in the fulfillment of the divine purposes in creation. Everyone within the community, like the members of the heavenly choirs and angelic orders, would have a place and a function. The town would be self-sufficient and free from the distractions and dissension of foreigners and aliens.

Of course, in an effort to maintain the ideal, admission to the city would be restricted to those with the proper qualifications. Just as the

Christian life was the price of admission to Augustine's City of God, so there were restrictions on the admission to the ideal city.

The Italian cities tended to extend citizenship on a very exclusive basis. One had to be of the city and had to pass stiff qualifications to be considered a citizen and enjoy the rights and responsibilities of citizenship. The town elites believed that citizenship, like salvation, separated the inhabitants of the city from those without, from the foreigners and aliens who would most certainly, if admitted, contaminate the chosen few, the citizens of the ideal city.

Finally, it must not be forgotten that the city had a purpose. The city would exist for the good of all and for the right of its inhabitants to live in peace and harmony.

Needless to say, medieval intellectuals experienced difficulty in reconciling the obvious contradictions between the ideal city and the realities of the towns in which they lived. But this is not to say that progress could not and was not being made. There were a number of factors working on behalf of the local elites who were seeking to implement environmental or quality-of-life legislation.

First, scholastic literature clearly reflects the willingness of the educated classes to take over and restructure biblical, classical, and other medieval literary models and apply them creatively to purposes heretofore unknown or to rework existing theories within the context of new information.

Second, there was a distinctive and acceptable contemporary intellectual process that permitted the inclusion and restructuring of concepts and theories of others into contemporary literary, religious, philosophical, and practical literature. The examples of Christian writers routinely adapting Platonic, Stoic, Hebraic, and Islamic intellectual constructs to the goals and ends of Christianity are legion.

Third, those responsible for the education and training of the secular elites and literate classes came from the same intellectual tradition as those responsible for the education and training of the religious elite. Hence, the educated tended to share common images, visions, and intellectual and linguistic constructs.

Fourth, the secular elites and their statute makers, notaries, and legal experts shared a disposition to combine the concepts and interests of church and state in their official actions, despite a nagging tradition of jurisdictional disputes over their respective sovereignties. The so-called Sacred Statutes, applying secular power to such religious issues as blasphemy, religious holidays, and the operation of church charities, found their way into statute collections alongside similar secular issues like perjury or working on Sundays or feast days. The civil enforcement of religious regulations demonstrates that there was a measure of toleration for religion in the town's civic life. It also could be argued that the inclusion of statutes of a religious nature in municipal statute collections implied that the religious/philosophical concepts of stewardship, a planned abode, and the ideal city were also influencing the direction in which the elites were leading their towns.

Fifth, the development and implementation of purely environmental legislation clearly demonstrates that the town elites were able to convert purely theoretical intellectual models into operational codes that regulated human behavior to the ends specified in the models.

And given the above, there is little doubt that the elites had the theory and the intellectual models that allowed them, if they so chose, to utilize an entire statute collection to legislate into existence a model of the "ideal city." But is there any evidence that such a project was actually undertaken?

Many of the statute collections themselves stand as mute evidence of a desire to provide for the orderly and comprehensive organization of those towns. In their completeness and their attention to detail, they represent clear attempts to provide for a respectable quality of life, a working economy, adequate security, the efficient delivery of municipal service, and a satisfactory working arrangement between the citizens and their governments. These officials never attained the ideal city, but they made the medieval city a much better place in which to live.

3

Regulating the Land

Until the products of Roman military and civil engineering genius began to make their appearance in those portions of the Mediterranean world controlled by Roman arms, the word "road" meant little more than a leveled track that wound its way around water holes and towns by the easiest gradients and pathways possible. By modern standards, the vast majority of pre-Roman roads would be considered little more than footpaths or bridle paths generally unsuited for wheeled traffic or large, bulky, transported loads of any sort. There were, however, some notable exceptions (such as the Greek "sacred roads,"[1] or the Persian Royal Road,[2] which stretched from Sardis to Susa), where a heavy volume of traffic for religious or military reasons required a wider or better-maintained roadway.

Historical Antecedents

The art of road building in the classical era reached its highest point with the Romans. The Roman road system, designed to meet the military necessity of tying together the far-flung corners of the empire, began with the Via Appia. This gravel-topped roadway,[3] linking Rome with Capua, was completed in 312 B.C.E. under the direction of the censor, Appius Claudius. Road building continued unabated on the Italian peninsula until 200 B.C.E., when the roads linking together all of the neighboring cities were substantially completed. This road-building effort was extended into Dalmatia in 145 B.C.E., to Asia Minor in 130 B.C.E., to southern Gaul in 120 B.C.E., and to the outer periphery of the Roman Empire during the first two centuries of the new era.

Unfortunately, by the fourth century, the Roman road system began to fall into disrepair as a series of imperial laws designed to require landowners whose properties adjoined the imperial roadways to provide for the maintenance of the roads and bridges. The policy proved to be miserably inadequate.[4]

Roman Road Construction

Roman roads were generally constructed according to a uniform pattern. Engineers first surveyed a route that was as close to a straight line as possible—a route that marched across the landscape making minimal concessions to topography and geography. First, furrows, called *sulci,* were dug out along each side of the proposed roadbed. They served both to mark out the roadway and, where necessary, to drain the roadbed. Next, a row of curbstones, or *umbones,* was set into each furrow. Laborers, under the direction of military engineers, then excavated the soil between the furrows. This excavation was then backfilled with distinctive layers of materials that included, from bottom to top, a layer of mortar on top of coarse sand, slabs or blocks of stone set in the mortar, and a layer of concrete containing crushed stone. This material was then tramped down and leveled to provide a lap, or *gremium,* onto which the fitted blocks, cobbles, or slabs, which formed the actual road surface, were set in mortar. This top layer was raised slightly in the center, or crowned, to force the rainwater into the ditches at the sides of the roadway. Any spaces left between the stones were filled with smaller stones or small bits of scrap iron, which were firmly mortared into place.[5]

In Italy, Roman roads were rarely raised on embankments except in marshy areas where the need for dry pavement dictated such construction. The convenience of local landowners, whose property abutted the roadway, was also an important consideration, although cost-conscious engineering contractors could not ignore the fact that an elevated roadway required more maintenance due to excessive erosion and additional construction costs were incurred to build ramps at those sites where local roads and byways crossed the main roadway. In the provinces, these niceties were not always observed and because of the need for speedy construction or because of a lack of precise knowledge of subsoil conditions, roadways were frequently raised or elevated on embankments.

Secondary roads were clearly distinguished from the primary or paved roadways (*via lapide strata*), which were usually found (with some notable exceptions) only in Italy or at the approaches to major cities where heavy traffic and dust necessitated pavements. Sanded or graveled roadways (*via glarea strata*) were the norm outside of Italy and in the more remote areas. These roads were about six meters wide (around 19.7 feet) and their surfaces were also crowned. The road itself usually consisted of a thick layer of gravel laid over a layer of heavier stones rammed into the subsoil.

Since the primary purpose of Roman roads was to provide for efficient communications between the various local, provincial, and central government administrative centers, the roads, or *cursus publici*, were maintained at government expense. In addition to the roads themselves, post stations (for changes of horses and wheeled vehicles) and rest houses (*mansiones*) were situated and maintained at convenient locations with government funds for the use of those on public business. Private individuals, however, had to make their own arrangements at the frequently disreputable, citizen-owned inns.

Roman bridges connecting these roads remain even today some of the most important monuments to Roman technical competence. Bridges were designed and constructed to meet the specific needs of each site, and as a result, the construction materials employed differed from bridge to bridge just as they did for the roads. Roman engineers built some bridges completely out of stone, others from timber and stone, and still others wholly of timber. Most surviving Roman bridges have brick-faced, semicircular concrete arches, varying in span from 5 to 20 meters (from around 16.4 to 65.6 feet), which were set in concrete piers that were faced with large stones or brick. Half-timber bridges had wooden superstructures set in brick or stone-faced concrete piers. These piers usually had cutwaters on the upstream side to divert water and ice. The approaches to bridges were on earthen embankments that were sometimes riveted in stone or brick. In general, the durability of these bridges, just like the roads, has more than amply testified to the competence of Roman engineers.

Early Roman bridges and roads were generally built by the army to accommodate the special requirements of military transport. This back-breaking labor was never particularly welcomed by the legions and their non-Roman auxiliaries; and because the use of regular troops only too frequently led to mutiny,[6] Roman military commanders resorted to the use of slave or forced-labor battalions. By 200 B.C.E, civilian authorities, looking for a more efficient way to extend the road system, began to take this task over from the military. They, in turn, let contracts out to civilian builders who erected or maintained the roads.[7]

Government Responsibility for the Roads

Early in Roman history, the roads were supervised by volunteer officials and rich private individuals whose rewards for such service included the right to name the roads after themselves or to erect triumphal arches. Special officers, called *curatores viarum*, were appointed at a later time to oversee the roads under senatorial supervision, but as road-related legislation increased in complexity, permanent boards, or *curatores viae*,[8] were appointed by the emperor to oversee the building and repair of these roads.

Financing the roads was always a difficult problem. Whereas the earliest roads—as was fitting given their military purposes—were paid for out of the booty from successful military campaigns, this source of income rapidly dried up and alternate sources of funding had to be located. In 111 B.C.E., an agrarian law required those living along the roadways to pay for the upkeep of the roads abutting their property. As noted earlier, republican and imperial officials (and even the emperor himself) were required to pay for repairs and maintenance at their own expense. On occasion, direct taxes were levied for this purpose.[9] Towns were also sometimes permitted to levy tolls on the roads within their vicinity to pay for road maintenance.[10]

Roman municipal law provided a model that was adopted by most of the towns subject to imperial control. In Rome, and later elsewhere, each householder was charged with the responsibility of maintaining that portion of the roadway that passed the household.[11] The aediles, in turn, enforced this law. If a roadway passed by a public building or a temple, the public treasury absorbed the cost; in cases where the street passed between a temple and a private residence, the cost was shared equally between the private owner and the public treasury.[12] So that the maintenance of the roadway would be on a uniform basis, home owners probably paid a flat rate to the public authorities, thereby discharging their personal liability. Given this policy, the aediles acquired the additional responsibility of issuing contracts for the maintenance and repair of the local roadways and of overseeing the contractors' work to insure the quality and quantity of their efforts.

The Roman road system began to decline during the second century, and this decline was hastened by official abuse and the imperial decision to provide for roadway maintenance through compulsory service and payments. Municipal authorities, already overburdened by increasing workloads and other demands on their financial resources, failed to enforce existing laws and require property owners to perform required maintenance services. At the same time, imperial fiscal policies gradually dried up the regular sources of income and eliminated that means of roadway support.

Breakdown of the Roads

The dissolution of centralized Roman authority under the impact of successive waves of barbarian invasions after the fourth century also meant the collapse of the remaining road-building and maintenance activities. Without repairs and with the encroachments of landowners and the depredations of people seeking building materials, Roman roads rapidly became impassable to normal traffic in many areas, although they were still used by a limited number of travelers, pilgrims, merchants, and messengers. Most of these people walked, although horses, mules, and donkeys were becoming more commonplace as time wore on.

During the centuries before the first millennium, road building and maintenance remained in theory the responsibility of the local landowner, but these obligations were generally ignored.[13] As a result, compulsory labor was used where keeping roads and bridges in good repair appeared expedient. Some measure of success was obtained in and near the cities because of the denser populations and the necessities of increased trade after the year 1000 due to the Italian Commercial Revolution. Tolls and taxes were frequently levied to provide a financial basis for these repairs.

As urban governments began to develop increasingly effective control over their environs during the eleventh and twelfth centuries, they began to create communal statutes that afforded the elites a greater and more sophisticated measure of control over the local roads. Therefore, landowners protested the fines they received for failing to maintain the roadways adjacent to their lands, although on other occasions they begged local authorities to build and maintain toll roads. Money given by individuals, church organizations, or municipalities for the maintenance of bridges and roads often acquired a religious connotation, since many people believed that this service was true charity directed toward the unfortunate, that is, the traveler.[14] For example, the *Congregation of the Hospital of the Pontifical Brothers* was founded in the twelfth century to serve as bridge builders in Italy and France.[15] Gradually, however, laymen learned the bridge-building and road-repairing techniques and took over many of the responsibilities of the religious orders. Nonetheless, the work retained its religious character and religious authorities frequently granted indulgences and other spiritual inducements to those working on roads.[16]

These activities were not without results. By the end of the eleventh century, many of the Roman roads were repaired, and the trade routes over the Alps were restored. But the nature of the roadways was also changing. The older Roman roads were primarily intended to be military or post roads. Newer roads were repaved with the intent that the roadways be widened to accommodate wheeled traffic; they were paved with cobbles or broken stone over a loose foundation of sand, a surface that had the advantage of being easily repaired and was less susceptible to the expanding and contracting action of heat and cold. The cobbles or stones were frequently cemented into place with a mortar consisting of a mixture of lime, river mud, and sand.

The Medieval Roadway

Within the cities and towns of Roman Italy, streets tended to be narrow by modern standards[17] because the ancients felt a need to be sheltered from the winds, which they believed carried dangerous humidity and diseases.[18] The streets were paved with squared stones (*peperini*), rectangular basalt slabs, or silex. During the imperial period, the adoption and widespread use of the peristyle house led to the development of narrow, arcaded streets. Because wheeled transportation within the city, except during clearly defined periods, was discouraged or even forbidden, home owners would frequently barricade streets with chains or stepping stones.

A Caesarean law of 47 B.C.E. provided legal inducements to municipalities to pave their streets, to prohibit the disposal of trash in the streets and public byways, and to provide for their regular cleaning with water. By the time of Augustus, the widths of the municipal roadways were set by decree[19] and pedestrians were allotted walkways, which were to be eleven to seventeen inches wide and clearly marked by curbstones. These walkways were interrupted at frequent intervals by drains that led from structures abutting the roadway to closed sewers.

The streets themselves were drained by methods first developed by the Etruscans; these drains were usually covered trenches set beneath the pavement.[20] Roman municipal codes generally specified that drains from private housing and public structures alike had to lead directly into the street drains and usually had to be covered. The prevalence of running water in the households and public facilities of many of the larger cities during the imperial period provided an adequate flowage to remove waste, although in smaller towns and cities where the amenity of household running water was not quite as prevalent, seasonal rains provided the routine cleansing action in those towns whose municipal codes did not provide for periodic waste disposal by other methods. Many Roman streets were well lit by the time of the Roman Empire, although it was not uncommon for nocturnal travelers to be accompanied by armed bodyguards or slaves bearing lanterns.[21]

As the imperial authority of the Roman state declined during the fourth and fifth centuries, there was a corresponding decline in the corporate authority of the local municipalities. By the year 1000, the decline of municipal authority was almost complete. Refuse was thrown into the streets, and although laws requiring home owners to clean up the areas in and about their households remained on the books, they were seldom enforced. Some towns were cleaned thoroughly only as preparation for visiting dignitaries or on some seasonal basis. Many towns also required their citizens to clean the areas in front of their homes on a weekly basis. These laws were rigidly enforced in many towns,[22] although in others, home owners were assisted in this task by the considerable numbers of half-wild pigs that wandered about foraging in the rubbish.[23] This would remain the case until the later Middle Ages, when towns began to hire and maintain crews of scavengers, street cleaners, and garbagemen.[24] Rubbish not removed by natural means was carried out by hand or in wheelbarrows (invented in the thirteenth century) to the rivers or dunghills located outside the city walls.

Drainage in the medieval town tended to be far removed from the Roman model. The sewer was frequently little more than an open cut, or *clavus*, or a channel in the middle of the street, which, in addition to being the receptor for raw household sewage, also became a convenient refuse dump. In some towns, small streams or rivers were diverted into the local sewer system or individual sewer lines to flush them out. That this approach to urban sanitation was less than ideal needs no further elaboration here.[25]

Road surfaces, even in the larger cities,[26] continued to be a problem during the first centuries of the new millennium. Paving applied during the Roman period had in many areas simply disappeared. Civil authorities throughout Europe pressured local property owners to maintain the roadways adjoining their property, usually at their own expense, although there were numerous examples of tolls being levied on vehicles and goods to pay for repaving.[27]

Paving technology also changed after the eleventh century. Most paving projects, whether for roads, town squares, or marketplaces, utilized sand as a base; gravel tended to be used on roadways, whereas squares and markets were paved with cobbles. Repairs were very simple. Potholes were simply filled with scrap lumber and wood chips. When roads were resurfaced, the old surface was rarely removed; rather, a new set of cobbles or gravel was laid and compacted with hand rams. This frequently resulted in the roadways themselves being raised. As a result, legislation occasionally appeared requiring residents to "level," or perhaps, "lower," roadways, since, as noted previously, these raised roads were more susceptible to erosion or breakaway damage and there were difficulties associated with the approaches to those roadways. At times, the roads were "raised," but this type of construction was generally associated with areas with drainage problems or with roads located along rivers with potential flooding problems.

The most serious damage to the roadways has been attributed to encroachments by home owners and by heavy vehicular traffic. Town officials issued a series of laws to curb the tendency of property owners to obtain the maximum use of scarce urban land at the expense of the roadways, but apparently, inadequate enforcement and small fines were ineffective deterrents. Iron-shod cart wheels caused the most serious damage to the roadways. When legislation was passed forbidding iron-shod wheels, wheels were studded with round-headed nails. These new wheels created even more havoc and they, too, were banned. Nails were no longer allowed unless they were of the flat-headed variety. But even this tactic was unsuccessful. Finally, wheels clad with any form of metal were banned. And laws restricting when and where wheeled traffic would be permitted proliferated, but all such laws were broken wherever and whenever it seemed expedient, sometimes with impunity, as some communal officials failed to enforce these statutes because of the needs of commercial activities resident in the towns. Traffic continued to increase, with resultant traffic jams at the toll gates, and lawsuits over traffic accidents, reckless driving, and speeding became epidemic.[28]

Medieval Urban Waste Management

Refuse and Animal Waste Products

The problem of litter within the medieval city, like its modern counterpart, was monumental. The litter problem was further complicated by a lack of space within the walls and by the lack of a common procedure for the removal and disposal of trash and garbage. Each of the northern Italian cities had, at some point, passed legislation designed to control the problem, but the problem persisted, as did the legislation against it.

The medieval Italian town, by virtue of its construction, sources of power, and resource base, was almost completely dependent upon nature. Thus, much of its refuse and waste materials were of organic origin.

Plant refuse abounded in the medieval city. Large amounts of hay, straw, and other grass-related fodder were stored, but fodder storage generated dust and chaff and created fire problems. As a result, the possession of fodder was banned for all except those who owned horses, cattle, or other hay-consuming animals. The amount was generally limited to a "one day and one night supply."[29] Building supplies, especially reeds, planks, and lumber, tended to clutter the streets and byways of towns both during construction and afterward. Individual property owners as well as construction contractors had to be reminded by the force of law to clean up after themselves.[30] Bassano was perhaps more stringent than most towns in warning its inhabitants that lumber and other construction materials could not be stored in the town's streets or porticos (whether on the ground or in wagons) for more than a single night.[31] Refuse was a road-related problem precisely because of the failure of individual citizens, contractors, and businessowners to clean up during the course of their daily activities. These piles of refuse created blockages within the town's traffic arteries, which in turn had a negative impact upon the town's merchants, industrialists, and other large-scale businesspeople whose economic (and perhaps political) survival depended upon the free movement of goods and services through the community.

The presence of animals within the medieval town was a necessary nuisance. Animals passing through the town or stabled therein dropped waste matter everywhere. Stable hands and others who cleaned out the stables, pens, and other enclosures would sweep the accumulated droppings, straw, and other stable waste into the street, where it would no longer be their responsibility. This problem could be alleviated in two ways: first, by limiting the number of animals, and second, by requiring prompt cleanup.

Although there does not appear to have been a substantial body of legislation specifically limiting the numbers of draft animals, horses, or cattle that an individual could keep in town, medieval authorities placed other types of restrictions upon animal owners. For example, Bassano did not permit anyone to own horse-drawn transportation or to drive a wagon through the town on Sunday before the ninth hour.[32] The city fathers also enacted laws that prevented local herdsmen from buying foreign animals to increase the size of their herds[33] and from allowing their animals to run freely through the city.[34] Dogs and cats were also required to be kept in pens at their owners' homes.[35] Verona passed similar restrictions against herdsmen, wagoneers, and others wishing to pass through the town,[36] as well as against those who wanted to keep pigs[37] or sell animals within the town limits.[38] Restrictions on the activities of contractors and the sellers of foodstuffs tended to limit the amount of time that they could keep draft animals within the town walls.

Almost every town required that animal wastes be cleaned up within a reasonable time.[39] Although it appears that this material, which included straw, hay, and other waste materials found in stables, pens, and the like, was generally swept up, put into wheelbarrows and similar conveyances, and removed to dumps and refuse heaps beyond the town walls, some towns devised other solutions. Spoleto, for example, arranged that animal wastes from the captain's stables should be delivered to the Brothers of the Order of the Sacked Friars,[40] presumably for fertilizer (similar to modern organic lawn fertilizers).

Human Waste Products

The problem of disposing of human waste has always been a serious environmental concern in human communities, past and present. Thus, it is hardly surprising that it has been a frequent consideration of urban legislation.[41]

In terms of roadways, medieval legislation was aimed at keeping the roadways free of sewage. The purpose of such legislation was generally twofold. First, because most medieval housing did not have indoor plumbing, the prevalent waste receptacle was the chamber pot, and the most convenient form of disposal was out the nearest window or doorway.[42] This Bassano law is typical of legislation designed to prevent this type of abuse: "We decree that no one should throw water, offal, or any other waste or harmful materials from their homes, or outside of their homes, onto the level places on the road or in the porticos, or to make water in a portico or a ditch."[43]

It is interesting to note that a distinction was made between human and animal waste product removal. For example, whereas Bassano adopted numerous measures against human waste being dumped into the streets or against people who relieved themselves in the streets or public buildings, the code allowed stable owners to sweep out their stables and leave the refuse in the streets for up to five days.[44]

Some indication of the attitude of medieval townspeople toward the problem of the elimination of human waste products from the streets can be obtained by investigating other measures contained in the legislation. The Piranese Law Code of 1307 lumps together "filth, sour wine, or any garbage."[45] Bassano[46] and Bologna,[47] among other cities, routinely included references to human wastes with wastewater, garbage, straw, or litter. The implication is that human waste products were viewed as simply another form of litter blocking free access to the town's roadways and were not seen as posing any real health concerns.

Industrial Waste Products

Another form of waste was the by-products of industrial production. Industrial wastes (which are addressed in Chapter 6 as an environmental problem affecting the quality of life in the city as a whole) were treated in the same manner as human, animal, or plant wastes, namely, their presence on the street constituted an impediment to the free use of the streets. For this reason, those who caused or were responsible for the industrial wastes were enjoined to prevent such wastes from reaching the streets, but if they did cover the streets or impede the traffic, those responsible were required under legal penalties to clean up the mess that was made.[48]

Legislation

If sanitation, health considerations, or merely the need to control the more noxious odors was not the primary goal of this legislation, what was the intent of the statute makers? In 1301, Bassanese statute makers indicated that it was "nevertheless understood that the (construction) materials must be left in such a way that men can conveniently go through the streets and porticos with persons, horses, and wagons."[49] In another statute from the same codification, home owners were enjoined to keep the roads clear of debris so that "travelers can come and go comfortably."[50] In Spoleto, the city fathers authorized the diverting of a river so that a roadway could be used and the commune would not suffer the continued loss of vital food supplies;[51] and in another chapter of their statutes, they ordered the walling up or covering over of sewer outfalls and drains so that "filth would not cover the road."[52] Veronese statute makers insisted that all sewer drains be covered and that sewage be directed away from the streets; the only exceptions to this rule were those drains and outfalls that emptied directly into the River Adige.[53] Ferranese law makers enacted the following statute in 1287:

> We decree and ordain that, since it is useful to all of the districts of the Commune of Ferrara, [it is understood] that each district of the City of Ferrara, which has a road to the Po, is obliged to construct at the expense of all of the men living in the aforesaid districts one road of squared blocks, which are three feet square, and the roadway should be more than ten feet wide and should extend all the way to the Po, so that the men and women of the district can come and go freely to get water, wood, hay, straw, wine, and certain foods.[54]

Thus, it would appear that the primary concern of the urban lawmakers was to keep the roads passable for ordinary traffic. By the same token, one should not assume that they were not also interested in keeping their cities clean. Indeed, nearly every town passed a law similar to the following: "I [each citizen] will see to it that the City is cleaned of filth and dirt once a year and that garbage is not thrown into the porticos, roads, and streets."[55]

The responsibility for the cleaning process normally rested on the shoulders—and dipped into the pocketbooks—of the home owners or landowners whose properties abutted the roadways. This responsibility was shared with the commune government only occasionally and then in situations clearly spelled out in the statutes themselves. For example, one Ferrara statue read: "We decree and ordain that roads made of squared blocks should be repaired at the expense of local districts in which they are located if they should in any way be damaged. And the Judge of the Embankments of Ferrara is obliged to take care of this on each Kalends."[56] Some towns also realized that the annual cleanups were not enough and passed legislation requiring biennial, then seasonal, and, finally, more frequent cleanups.[57]

A further indication of the desire of the city fathers and the statute makers to promote ease of movement through their towns by way of the road systems is indicated by the frequency of the legislation requiring the repair, maintenance, leveling, raising, and resurfacing of the towns' roads.

Road repair legislation generally takes one of several forms: The roads were to be leveled or raised, resurfaced with gravel, or repaved with squared blocks or other forms of stone. The most common form of repairs or maintenance called for in the legislation was for the leveling or raising of roadways.[58] Unpaved roads became rutted and uneven as a result of heavy traffic, weather, flooding, and other natural occurrences; and repairs sought to promote better drainage and ease of travel. Some roads were raised, leveled, or received a layer of gravel or crushed local rock.[59] Other roads, presumably those more heavily traveled or in areas that because of ceremonial functions, required a more durable and serviceable surface, were paved with squared stone or cobbles.[60] Statute makers did not often provide the rationale for these road-building or road-maintenance projects, but when they did, reasons such as the following were offered:

> that men should be able to go through the porticos;[61] [roads should be so constructed] that two wagons, while passing one another, can not become mired there;[62] the person who destroyed the roadway or raised it too little is

obliged to level the road so that water might have a free downflow and that no water therefrom might cause a loss;[63] that roads should not be narrowed or damaged because of sewer construction;[64] the road . . . should be leveled and raised two feet so that carts and horses can freely use it and the [banks of the] canal should be raised so that it does not flood the road;[65] and the road should be repaired . . . since neither wagon, knight, nor footsoldier can pass by that roadway.[66]

Finally, an explanation for the apparently extensive damage to the various roadways not attributable to the normal wear and tear caused by regular road use can be summed up in a single thought: The commune simply did not enforce its own laws effectively. Included in the extensive Ferrarese statute collection is the following unusual and enlightening explanation for a road clearance and maintenance project in the community:

It is understood that the custom and measure for those roads which has been set down in the books of the statutes of the Commune of Ferrara should be maintained so that the aforesaid road should not henceforth be cluttered since this trespass has happened only too frequently because of impiety and the lack of punishment in the City of Ferrara and the Commune.[67]

In addition to antilitter and ease of movement considerations, road-related legislation also dealt with the problem of flood control. In Spoleto, the River Saletto overflowed its banks and washed out a key roadway used to bring food into the city from the surrounding countryside. Furthermore, the roadway could not be repaired because the river had cut a new bed through portions of the roadway. The podesta was instructed to assemble all those persons who were suffering losses and, from their number, to appoint two men; they would then have the authority to tax those affected by the floodwater and oversee the rerouting of the riverbed and the rebuilding of the roadway. Thus, the city fathers were quite willing to alter the natural environment to prevent further losses to the local property owners, but even more important, they wanted to maintain free access and passage along a vital roadway.[68]

Ferrara also had problems with waterways and roads. Some roads were used to channel local drainage systems, and when they fell into disrepair and the waters from the ditches caused losses, the local inhabitants were required to pay for the repairs.[69] On occasion, the commune had to take action to protect the roads from flood damage,[70] and the reasons given, when they are cited, are usually to protect the surrounding properties and to keep the roadways open to regular traffic.

The Bolognese statute collection contains a provision enjoining house-holders and others to see to it that ditches, sewers, and drains were not cut across roadways but rather were buried or covered over "so that anyone might be able to come and go."[71]

Ferrara was also concerned about pedestrian traffic. The Ferrarese statute makers enacted a statute in which they decreed that "footpaths should be made four episcopal feet wide from twenty miles outside of the City and they should be kept mowed and brush should be removed from them at the wish of the Council and they should be cleared and kept clean."[72] The same consideration applied to the footpaths that generally applied to the roads, namely, that the local authorities were obliged to keep them clear, clean, and passable.

Conclusion

The environmental concerns expressed in the road-related legislation were quite straight forward. The roads had to be kept clean and free of debris, refuse, and garbage; the primary reason for this appears to be the communal government's interest in keeping the roads clear for pedestrian and vehicular traffic. This concern was also reflected in the commune's concern for keeping the roads paved. Wheeled traffic was also restricted in some towns. Damaged roads were to be repaired immediately by those who damaged them or by those who lived near them. Even floodwaters, a river that had moved out of its bed, canals, sewers, and ditches had to be diverted to protect the roads; the roads themselves also had to be raised and leveled to ward off water damage. Sewers and drains that approached roads had to be covered over or buried as necessary to maintain free and easy passage.

However, there does not appear to be any real concern routinely ex-pressed in the laws about sanitation or environmental issues in the mod-ern sense. In those laws relating to road-building or maintenance, the statute makers did not consider that garbage, refuse, or stable litter would cause disease or other medical problems. Perhaps the closest they came to expressing environmental awareness in the modern sense was in the rela-tively strong and expressive language (e.g., *putredo*, meaning something putrid) used to refer to sewage waste and in the detailed terminology used to describe other kinds of waste. By separating the waste into categories, they were at least coming to a realization that the problem of waste was not some formless, shapeless mass to be dealt with by generic legislation, but rather they acknowledged that the problem had any number of specific causes, each of which had to be considered if the problem was going to be effectively handled. For example, lawmakers tended to be far more concerned about confining human waste products to covered sewers and drains (and keeping them off the streets) than they were about animal droppings, which, given the number of animals required by the medieval town's economy, had to create an infinitely larger problem of disposal. And yet, some towns permitted stable owners to leave the stable sweepings in the street for as long as five days. Perhaps, in this differentiated treatment of the various species of waste lies the beginning of an environmental awareness—an awareness that there was something unhealthy in the streets that could afflict the population.

4

Protecting the Water

An adequate supply of safe drinking water was central to the survival of any town in any era of human history. Although cities have sometimes been able to survive and perhaps even prosper without adequate food supplies, metals, minerals, or other resource bases, no city in history has long survived the demise of its water supply.

Ancient Water and Sewer Systems

In classical times, the development of urban water supplies generally centered around dependable sources such as rivers, streams, or wells.[1] Wells have long been considered a characteristic of urban areas or any other area with a concentrated population. These wells were routinely dug by hand rather than drilled, and they were lined with casings of wood, stone, brick, or with concrete linings. Water was extracted from the wells with gourds, shell dippers, pottery jugs, or buckets, and in the case of particularly deep wells, by water-lifting machinery that ranged from simple counterweighted buckets to treadmill-driven bailers, toothed wheels, or Archimedean screws. Once the water was drawn, it was generally stored in cisterns hewed from living rock or in masonry or brick structures that had barrel vaults, pillars, and settling tanks.

Where wells and other local sources of water were either not available or their water was not potable, water had to be imported from more distant sources. Contrary to popular belief, the majority of most aqueducts were underground rather than above ground. The *qanat* aqueduct, perhaps the oldest type in use, was little more than a mine shaft driven through a mountain to bring water from an otherwise inaccessible site to a distribution point by the shortest route possible. The water line approaching the adit was probably a pipeline supported by stones. When steep valleys had to be crossed, a siphon was used to lift the water. The problem with siphon-based systems was that the existing technology was not adequate to overcome the difficulties involved in developing tubes and pipes capable of withstanding the high pressure at the base of the siphon without undue water loss. Tunnels and siphons were the norm for most of the Greek, and later, the Hellenistic, city-state water systems.

In the centuries between the founding of the cities of the biblical Middle East and the imposition of the Pax Romana upon the peoples of the Mediterranean Basin, there were few advances in the technology of bringing water into urban areas. Aqueducts were still the primary man-made means of bringing water into many Roman cities. Whether intended to carry water for public use (such as for the flushing of sewers, or for baths, lavatories, and fountains) or for private use (such as for homes and mills), these aqueducts were usually built and maintained at public expense.[2] The administration of the municipal water systems proved to be an efficient function of local government until the later days of the Roman republic when political upheavals ushered in a period of neglect during which some of the aqueducts were allowed to fall into disrepair and private interests were able to utilize the municipal water systems at the expense of the general public.

After the fall of the republic, successive imperial administrations made the rehabilitation of existing aqueducts, the construction of new aqueducts, and the restoration of municipal water systems high-priority public projects. Imperial reforms, however, were not directed solely at the redevelopment of the physical resources of the local water systems but also sought to improve the administration of those services. Whereas municipal water systems had been routinely administered by the local magistrates under the republic, reform-minded imperial officials oversaw the development of commissions or boards that were made responsible for maintaining a safe and potable supply of water for the towns under their control.[3] The membership of these commissions tended to include a ranking magistrate and technical advisors who administered the expenditure of funds and supervised the relatively large staff of technicians, professionals, and laborers responsible for the daily operation of the municipal water system. This model, based upon the experience of the imperial administration of the City of Rome, was exported throughout the Roman Empire and became the standard administrative practice employed to supervise the delivery of many necessary municipal services.

The sources of the water utilized by municipal water utilities ranged from potable springs and rivers to seawater and other sources of nonpotable water. Before being passed into the aqueduct system, water was led through settling tanks that were normally constructed with sloping floors designed to facilitate the cleansing action. The water was then directed into the aqueduct, which carried it to the various distribution points. These catch basins were not reservoirs or holding tanks but rather collectors that served to direct the water to the areas where it was needed. For example, mains leading from a single distribution tank would service fountains, public buildings, and baths, as well as private residences, industries, tenement houses, and the like. From such sources as the baths and public buildings, the water was directed over water-wheels used to power mills or other industrial or craft enterprises.

Although the mains were not supposed to be tapped for private use, emperors sometimes granted certain individuals or syndicates the right to tap the public water lines for personal or commercial use. Consumers were normally charged according to the gauge of the private delivery pipe,[4] and the integrity of the pipe system was maintained through periodic inspections and sealing by municipal officials. That this system was not foolproof and that much water was diverted illegally for private use was underscored by Frontinus, who sought to curtail the activities of dishonest water men, landed proprietors, and others who were diverting water for private use to such an extent that the public watercourses ran dry.[5]

Pure water was an important concern of Roman engineers and physicians alike. There appears to be evidence that some municipal authorities may have been aware of or at least suspected that the use of lead for the lining of cisterns or in the fabrication of pipes was a public health hazard. Unfortunately, the technology of the time offered few alternatives for the use of lead, and the efforts of engineers and water officials to keep the pipes and cisterns free of calcium and lead carbonate deposits may have unwittingly contributed to the ongoing problem of lead poisoning, which was caused by exposing the water passing through the conduits or cisterns to the lead-soldered joints or lead casings.

Methods for testing water purity were rather simple, as evidenced by this statement of Vitruvius:

> The water, being sprinkled over a vessel of Corinthian bronze [a gold-silver-copper alloy] or any other good bronze, should leave no trace. Or if water be boiled in a copper vessel and allowed to stand and then poured off, it will also pass the test if no sand or mud be found in the bottom of the copper vessel. Again, if vegetables boiled in the vessel are soon cooked, they will indicate that the water is good and wholesome.[6]

Then there was the tried-and-true method of dripping wine drop by drop into a container to determine the lime content of the water.

Once the purity of the water was determined, the processes of purifying the water ranged from simple exposure to sunlight and air to filtration through various substances, including wool, lengths of wick, and sand. Vitruvius recommended that water be percolated through several layers of sand to insure its purity.[7] And finally, there was always the most common and effective method, that is, the purifying additive, of which the most readily available was wine.

To insure the efficiency of their water systems and to make certain that contaminated water did not pollute pure water (at least, to the extent that contemporary technology permitted), Roman engineers built drainage systems so efficient that some still remain in use today. Sewers were frequently constructed under sidewalks and connected to public and private buildings by clay pipes. The sewers were generally six feet deep and constructed of stone and mortar. The tops of the sewers were fitted with some stone slabs that could be removed for repairs. The individual sewer lines connected to private residences or public facilities carried raw sewage through the municipal sewers, emptying it into *cloacae* (tunnels that were large enough for a man to walk upright in), which then carried the sewage under the city fortifications and down to a nearby river or swamp. Within the *cloacae*, iron grilles were installed to keep anyone from entering while allowing the water free egress.[8]

Maintaining these sewers and keeping them free of debris and silt was an extremely expensive undertaking. This cost was partially paid for by the treasury and by an assessment called the *cloacarium*.[9] During the republican period, the cleansing and maintenance of the sewers was entrusted to the aediles and censors; under the empire, this task was undertaken by appointed officials known as *cloacarium curatores*. The actual work of cleansing the sewers was performed by condemned criminals because of the inherent dangers, not the least of which were the presence of methane gas and the diseases that current medical practice associated with the "noxious odors and airs" emanating from the sewage.

The term *cloaca* was also frequently used in classical times to refer to the drains. In this context, "drains" meant sewer drains as well as systems of ditches, conduits, covered and uncovered pipes, and similar means of moving unneeded waters from one point to another. The Italian riverine system has many rivers like the Tiber, Adige, and the Arno that are unable to contain the springtime floods; as a result, they are characterized by periodic flooding and fairly extensive marshes located near the river mouths. The Roman solution to these problems was quite straightforward: channelize the rivers and drain the marshlands where feasible.

Inland fields that tended to flood and swamps that were associated with particular rivers were frequently drained by subterranean tunnels. The purpose of the vast majority of these projects was to increase the amount of arable acreage available within Italy proper. Roman engineers successfully drained Lake Fucinus,[10] Lake Valinus, and the Plain of Raete, the marshes outside of Ravenna,[11] Bologna, Piacenza, and Cremona. They also channelized the Adige between Ferrara and Padua, as well as long stretches of the Po River.[12]

Similar projects were undertaken outside of Italy as well. For example, Roman military engineers channelized one of the mouths of the Rhone River to insure regular delivery of supplies to the garrison town of Arles.[13] In Roman Britain, a system of dikes and canals was built to reclaim the fens and to protect the flatlands of The Wash from the sea. Similar canal-building projects were undertaken along the Dutch coast to minimize seasonal flood damage. Canals were dug to connect the Rhine and the IJssel Rivers, and a mole was laid to keep the floodwaters out of the Waal River. The Meuse and the Rhine Rivers were connected in 45 C.E. by a ship canal designed to afford safe passage to merchant shipping during stormy periods.[14]

Medieval Water and Sewer Systems

The dissolution of the central authority of the Roman imperial state brought with it the inability to generate sufficient public funds to maintain basic services. In the absence to a central authority, the duty of maintaining vital services fell on the shoulders of private citizens and local municipal authorities. Some aqueducts were maintained by bishops as early as the seventh century, but the majority of the towns were forced to rely upon rivers, springs, and wells instead. The poorer townspeople were required to draw their water from the private wells or cisterns, or they had to make use of public wells or fountains. In some cases, water was brought to private homes by professional water carriers; other private citizens, not as fortunate, drew their own water with a bucket or a windlass or by using a bucket with a counterweight.

Supplies of pure water declined. This problem was further complicated by the fact that many wells, designed to collect rainwater, were located in low-lying areas near latrines and cesspools. The result was an almost inevitable contamination. Epidemics spread quickly. The streets, which were drained by open gutters, received all sorts of refuse and excreta and tended to drain into these same low-lying areas.

By the eleventh century, town officials tended to be aware of the problems inherent in this situation and began to take corrective action. In addition to cleaning the streets, officials began to pipe water into the towns from outside sources by way of pipes and aqueducts to fountains or private cisterns. Too frequently, however, private individuals tapped into the mains and had to be legally restrained. Protection of muncipal water intake and drainage systems became the subject of numerous statutes contained in the law codes of northern and central Italian municipalities.

Roman drainage and irrigation projects and techniques expanded during medieval times. Cistercian monks pioneered the use of city refuse and sewage to fertilize farmland as early as 1150, and they also irrigated the meadowlands of Citeaux, France. Drainage programs were expanded in the Low Countries, especially near the mouths of the Rhine, Meuse, and Scheldt Rivers.

The majority of the land reclamation projects were undertaken by certain religious houses, notably those of the Benedictines, Premonstratensians or Norbertines (White Canons), and the Cistercians. In time, these skills were learned by laymen, who became especially prominent in the northern European projects. This skill was recognized throughout Europe, and foreign engineers, especially those from Holland, were frequently imported to assist in Italian dike construction and rehabilitation projects.

Dike construction and maintenance generally came to be considered a community obligation. The responsibility for the dike or embankment (or a section of it) was assigned to each landholding.

Medieval dikes and embankments were generally constructed on solid earthen foundations, carefully cleared of vegetation. The central core of this earthwork was composed of boulder clay, which had been tramped down and compacted by treading with oxen or horses. This clay core was then planted with a covering layer of grass that was supposed to be kept trimmed and free of brush and trees. The portion of the embankment facing the water was often further protected by layers of reeds and pile fences, or stone walls and bundles of branches. Canals or ditches were constructed on the landward side of embankments to carry off rainwater, seepage, and other waste water.

Legislation

The municipal codes of this period did not often make explicit reference to the particular sources of the water used by local citizens. As a result, few references identified a well, a stream, or some other waterway as being the source from which citizens drew their daily water supplies. It appears that a number of the towns were able to maintain in working order all or part of the earlier Roman water distribution systems. This would tend to explain a concern expressed in many of the law codes, namely, that municipal fountains, aqueducts, and their associated conduits should be kept in good repair and that their waters should not be diverted for private consumption.[15]

In those towns in which the municipal water system was not extensive or perhaps not accessible to the general populace, there appears to have been a heightened concern for the purity of the riverine water supply. For example, in thirteenth-century Ferrara, no mention was made of the maintenance of fountains or their related conduits. Several explicit references, however, underscored the local lawmakers' concern with maintaining the purity of the Po waters. For example, people working with flax were warned to process no more than was needed for their personal use,[16] and flax and hemp were not to be placed in the town's waterways.[17] The same code prohibited fishermen from cleaning their catch on the banks of the Po[18] and forbade leather workers (and presumably, butchers) from disposing of the waste products of their trade in the river's waters.[19] Several laws also cautioned local officials and citizens to refrain from and prevent others from disposing of human waste products in the town's ditches, streets, and sewers that flowed downward into the Po.[20] What the city fathers were attempting to accomplish might be deduced from the following passage: "For the better health of the men of the City of Ferrara and its suburbs and for the beauty of the City of Ferrara, we decree and ordain that two good men, both law-abiding, and one good notary skilled in the law, should be chosen for each quarter every six months."[21] The statute went on to instruct these men to see to it that the citizens, "whether lay or ecclesiastic," clean the town's ditches and sewers during each season and also "when there is sewage and filth in them and every week at the time established by the edict." The podesta was enjoined to fine those who did not comply, and his judgment was to be based on the investigations and written reports of those men who had been chosen for this purpose from each ward of the city.

Similar concerns were expressed in Verona. Public officials were obliged to see to it that the riverbed of the Fiumicello and the streambeds of its tributaries were kept unobstructed lest "its water not flow or that filth be caused."[22] Citizens were threatened with fines if they washed clothes or threw unclean things or filth into the waters and cisterns.[23] Various craftsmen were also forbidden to throw the waste products of their trades into the waters.[24] Home owners were also cautioned not to build privies or outhouses over the river.[25]

The introductory statement from a Veronese statute of 1276 gives as clear a statement as might be expected to explain the rationale of the city fathers in keeping the waterways clear of sewage, industrial waste, and filth:

> Since the water of the Masera is quite useful and well known, and since many persons, both native-born and foreigners, come and go to these waters for the sake of their bodily health, we decree and ordain that, on behalf of the honor and advantage of the Commune of Verona and of the persons coming to the aforesaid Masera, the Masera should be cleansed, repaired, and renovated for the Commune of Verona, to the extent that it seems expedient.[26]

This clear policy statement appears to be somewhat muddied by the provisos contained in the very next statute. As in previous statutes, citizens were warned against throwing all manner of waste products and materials into the River Adige during the day.[27] Waste disposal was specifically banned from the area upstream of the iron outflow of the bathhouse; but at the same time, the statute permitted the use of the river as a sewer during the nighttime hours without restrictions.

It would seem that the statute makers were contradicting themselves and bowing to the special needs of the various craft industries. A careful look at all of the legislation in the Veronese Code of 1276 that relates to the waterways, sewers, or similar conduits reveals a common thread. The statute makers were uniformly concerned with maintaining a "free downfall" for the water. "Dead water" was contrasted with "running water." For example, they permitted waste products to be thrown "into running water only."[28] The River Adige was characterized as being rapid flowing, and accordingly, wastes could be thrown into it "during the night." When one considers the concern expressed by the city fathers over wastes dumped into the Adige upstream of the outflow of the bathhouse (whose intake pipe had to be also located upstream of the outflow pipe), it becomes evident that the Veronese were aware of the deleterious effects of the wastes put into the river. But at the same time, they were convinced that the rapidly running water would purify itself through the action of the sun and the process of aerification, and if the problem was not resolved through these natural processes, the city fathers could rest assured that the problem would have been washed downstream by sunrise when their own citizens would use the river's water either in the bathhouse or as a source of drinking water.

Spoleto, which derived a large proportion of its potable water from the Vallocchia River by way of a series of aqueducts, passed legislation to insure that the water in the fountains was not polluted. One of the first tasks facing an incoming podesta was the appointment of a guardian for each of the city's fountains.[29] These guardians were charged with the responsibility of looking after the fountains and their attendant catch basins. Among their responsibilities, and those of other public officials who had been appointed to maintain city functions, was that of reporting "whomsoever [they might] find making filth in a fountain." In carrying out this responsibility, they were accorded "full trust" and garnered one-half the fine mentioned in the statute.[30]

There is little doubt that the purity of the water resource of the medieval Italian commune was a paramount consideration. Officials were enjoined to keep the fountains free of filth[31] and to prevent citizens from washing clothes therein.[32] Water itself could only be drawn with the permission of the local official in charge of the fountain,[33] and these officials were warned to protect the fountains with serrated bars and locked iron gates.[34] When new fountains are built[35] or repaired,[36] the cost of the project was to be borne by the people who would thus be served by the fountain, although the water itself remained a concern of the commune, which saw to its equitable distribution through its appointed officials.[37] Extreme and repeated concern was expressed by statute makers lest anyone tap into the conduits to make private water lines and thereby diminish or impede the commune's public supply to the fountains.[38]

Drainage Systems

Perhaps the most copious body of law in the Italian city codes is related to the primary function of a system of sewers, drains, and ditches designed to accommodate ordinary runoff. Concerns expressed by statute makers were rather routine under the circumstances. Where systems were nonexistent or inadequate, the statutes authorized the construction of new systems.[39] Existing drains, ditches, and sewers were to be cleaned of debris,[40] repaired,[41] or widened[42] to insure the appropriate flowage through the ditches. The maintenance work ranged from the removal of refuse and plant matter to rather extensive repaving projects. The cost of all of these projects, with certain exceptions,[43] was borne by neighbors or those who derived benefit from those systems.[44]

It is interesting to note that statute makers cited the convenience of travelers and the protection of roadways as a reason for construction or maintenance of drainage systems, but they would charge local property owners for the cost of these projects. No reference was encountered in the law codes under study to imposing a tax or toll on travelers or merchants specifically to maintain roads or drainage systems.

Another often-expressed concern of the statute makers was their unwillingness to permit their citizens to allow sewers or drains to dump filth onto the streets, byways, waterways, or private holdings of the commune. Wrongdoers were forbidden to redirect the drains[45] and were directed to stop dumping the polluting elements into the ditches.[46] Where the existing drain system was impractical, they were told to cover over the drains and direct their contents to areas less sensitive to public concern.[47] Thus, public officials appeared concerned with the health issue and anxious to ensure that the more noxious and odious forms of waste be removed from the city both for public-related reasons and to maintain the overall pleasant environment of the city.[48]

At the same time, statute makers and public officials were also interested in some projects that were more ambitious than simply removing runoff and sewage. For example, Spoleto authorized the podesta in 1296 to construct a ten-foot-wide ditch through a forest and adjacent arable lands not subject to the commune to drain a marsh and redirect part of the flow of a small river. It appears from the wording of the legislation that the purpose of the project was to drain the marsh and the lands of several villages situated along its route.[49] An unspoken but perhaps equally compelling reason was the development of more farmland to produce food for a city already quite concerned about its food supply.[50]

Flood Control

Periodic flooding was also an ongoing concern of municipal officials in many towns. Systems of ditches and dikes were the primary means of controlling the problem. The city fathers of Spoleto were not overawed at the prospect of altering the sources of rivers when they caused flooding within the city. When the River Saletto devastated portions of the district of St. Beroto and cut off a portion of the city's food supply, the podesta was required to see to it that the citizens of that district elected individuals who would relocate the course of the river, levy taxes for the cost of the project, and make sure that the river's new channel remained free of debris and garbage.[51] In a similar fashion, when the water of the Tesini River left its normal course, the podesta was obliged to restore the waterway to its normal bed, which flowed under the Bridge of St. George, and to charge the cost of this project to the commune.[52] Ferrarese public officials were aware that there was a serious potential for the Po River to flood, and they acted in a forthright manner. The statutes clearly stated that the ditches and sewers had to be kept clear and free of debris to permit the water a free downflow.[53] Officials were appointed and required to consult with both the council and the local inhabitants to determine "in what manner the water can be better conveyed and how the money which is necessary for this project should be assessed and imposed on those owners and neighbors."[54] The commune explicitly commanded its officials, especially those charged with the specific responsibility of overseeing the dikes and embankments, neither to accept bribes nor to undertake projects that were not consistent with the common good of the commune. Verona, in a similar manner, enacted legislation designed to warn its citizens not to tamper with, impede, or divert the water or watercourses of its rivers and streams, lest, in doing so, they cause a loss for property owners in the general vicinity.[55]

Ferrara's problem with flooding, however, was not a matter that could be handled effectively by the excavation of ditches and streambeds. As a result, Ferrara was forced to build an extensive system of dikes (or, at least, to maintain and extend the one that had been built by Roman engineers) to keep the Po within its banks. An extensive portion of the Ferrarese legal corpus was dedicated to the legal basis for this system of dikes and embankments. These structures were placed in the hands of a "judge of the embankments," who had the legal responsibility for maintaining them and their integrity.[56] He, in turn, was assisted by a corps of local district superintendents who were responsible to him and who were directed to assist him in the decisionmaking process.[57] The embankments themselves were given heavy legal protection to prevent anyone from breaching them or using their materials in local construction projects.[58] The embankments were to be kept clear of debris, trees, and bushes at all times,[59] lest their roots weaken the embankments or impede the efforts of those who would be shoring them up in time of flooding.

The cost of maintaining and extending these embankments must have been enormous, and the commune's concern for them apparently matched the expenditure. The actual financial cost was borne by the commune as well as by those who benefited.[60] But in addition to the financial commitments, the various districts protected by the dikes were required to furnish large amounts of manpower to work on them.[61] Given the amount of money and manpower involved in the undertaking, the potential for graft and corruption was extreme (similar in this way to other civic concerns such as weights and measures regulations). The statute makers recognized this potential and enacted specific legislation aimed at preventing officials from taking advantage of their position and preventing private individuals from profiting at public expense.[62]

Conclusion

There is little doubt that municipal officials realized that there was a relationship between good public health and safe drinking water supplies and public sanitation. Accordingly, they took pains to enact legislation that warned citizens not to throw odious or hazardous wastes into the water upon which their citizens depended. They were, however, less concerned about what went into the waterways downstream of their city. Even within the city, measures were enacted to protect the integrity of the water supplies and their systems of distribution from pollution or diversion. Clearly, the elites found it in their interest to protect the water supply from various types of pollution associated with industrial and commercial activities and from the by-products of human habitation, namely, sewage and garbage. The appropriate legislation was passed and appears to have been enforced. Whether this was done out of civic pride, economic self-interest (that is, the preservation of the health of the workforce or the military forces), or out of concern for their own health remains unclear.

Public sanitation was also a clear-cut concern. The legislation leaves little doubt that public officials were cognizant of the dangers inherent in allowing human, animal, and industrial waste products to remain within the town and its streets and byways. Hence, the desire to have open sewer lines covered, outfalls directed away from human contact, sewers and drains free and clear to permit a free downflow was clearly stated in this legislation. Even when wastes had to be contained within the city in cesspools, regulations were enacted to control the environment around them. Several laws clearly stated that their purpose in regulating the sewer or drainage system was a matter of public health.

Legislation enacted to prevent or limit flooding and the enormous amount of manpower and financial resources expended for this flood control is a clear statement of intent on the part of the city fathers to further insure a safe and healthy environment for the residents within their jurisdiction. Furthermore, the effect of the legislation was not only a matter of maintaining a safe environment for human habitation but was also geared toward providing commercial and industrial establishments with safe sites for their businesses and free and unencumbered access along communal roadways for the movement of raw materials, finished products, and food supplies for the workers. The sheer amount of this type of legislation underscores the seriousness of the statute makers' intent to afford residents a measure of security and protection that was not normally given in more rural environs. It also emphasizes their intent to enforce legislation that may have not been taken seriously by law enforcement personnel or by those who were bound by it.

All in all, this legislation is indicative of a firm resolve on the part of public officials (and those whom they represented) in this era to master their environment and to render their cities safe and desirable for human habitation and suitable for industrial and commercial activities.

5

Eliminating Wastes

For the historian seeking to explain complex processes and multifaceted causations, there is always the temptation to sort information, events, and people into those categories that render explanations that are clear and self-evident. The populations of medieval Italian towns present just such a dilemma. P. J. Jones, writing in the *Cambridge Economic History of Europe*, attempted to divide the residents of Italian towns into a number of socioeconomic categories ranging from noblemen to artisan to peasant.[1] Once these categories were established and defined, it was relatively easy to explain the motivation and activities of a particular class of urban residents in terms of their socioeconomic interests. Given this orientation, Jones was able to assert that the noble class enacted legislation that expressed its interests and that merchants and artisans, who were in control of a particular locale, passed legislation aimed at protecting their particular interests.

Trade-Related Legislation

But in the medieval Italian commune, such categories as notary, butcher, physician, or tanner simply do not hold up under scrutiny. Trades were often combined with other endeavors. The butcher might not only engage in that particular craft but might also own land outside the walls from which he might import livestock and agricultural products. A particularly successful clothier or leather worker might amass excess capital that he might then lend out at interest. In turn, success as a part-time moneylender might lead the same individual or perhaps another member of his household into banking. Such occupational crossover was one of the causes of the Italian Commercial Revolution and this form of activity sustained it for a long period of time. For example, churchman and physician were often the same person. Thus, class interests were often blurred by the competing demands of their different professions and occupations.

Trade-related legislation reflects the diversity of the interests of the people of the commune. The number of craftsmen or artisans serving in the commune's policymaking bodies was initially quite small, although their number in proportion to the total tended to increase dramatically by the thirteenth century.[2] Against the interests of noblemen and powerful commercial magnates, there developed the institution of the *societas popoli,* or the *popolo,* as discussed in Chapter 1.[3]

The *popolo,* with its political and military characteristics, evolved into a state within a state that successfully and frequently challenged the communal authority. As time passed, the *popolo* was able to secure for its members significant proportions of the voting memberships of the communal policymaking bodies. Economic and social pressure and compromise tended to limit confrontations between communal and popular authorities and to allow the political system to function.

The legislation that arose out of this tenuous and shifting relationship tended to reflect the changing priorities of communal and popular authorities. As a rule, the *popolo* sought to prevent, through constitutional legislation and penal codes, the magnates, nobility, and laboring classes from using their power to interfere with the political rights, personal immunities, and safety of the *popolani,* the members of the *popolo.* The *popolani* were also concerned lest restrictive legislation or confiscatory taxation prevent the legitimate use and enjoyment of their property, businesses, and the profits thereof. In the attainment of those goals, the guilds (fraternities of craftsmen) frequently exercised a surprising amount of control over the socioeconomic activities of their members, who, as a tightly knit group with significant economic resources, were often able to extend their control over the majority of the town's population. For example, in 1293, the Paduan guilds organized themselves into a single pressure group with the avowed intent of preventing their domination by any individual or faction. To attain these goals and to insure unanimity in their political activities, the guild of notaries, for instance, insisted that its members who sat on the council express only the views of the majority of the guild.[4] Environmental legislation relating to tradesmen should therefore be considered within the context of the ability of that pressure group to affect the content of legislation relating to their craft or trade. More precisely, the guilds wanted to influence the function and effect of communal legislation as it defined the manner in which public officials restricted tradesmen and the conduct of their business in the political attempt to protect the health, safety, and general environment of the city.

The Butcher and Meat Purveyor Guilds

Other than the goldsmiths' guilds (which exercised control over an obviously valuable commodity), two guilds, those of the butchers and the bakers, exerted an important measure of control over the socioeconomic and political activities of the commune by virtue of the products that they produced. Generally speaking, the ruling classes sought to regulate these guilds with the intent of insuring maximum production of the foodstuffs required by the local population at the lowest possible prices.

The communal authorities generally had a difficult time developing really effective controls over the butchers' guilds for economic reasons. The policymakers in the commune often had several objectives in mind when they enacted legislation, namely, the health of the population, the desire that the consumer not be cheated by artificially inflated prices or dishonest weights and measures, and the need to maintain the peace and tranquillity of their towns. Unfortunately, the good intentions of statute makers were frequently hampered by factors beyond their control, including the law of supply and demand, the need to retain the allegiance of the persons most often responsible for supplying foodstuffs for the towns' armed forces, and the tendencies within the guilds for restricted membership, occupational heredity, fraternal solidarity, and the acquisition of large amounts of excess capital.

The butchers' guilds generally sought to acquire power through the practice of cartel buying. The demand for meat products within the communes favored the guilds' efforts in this regard. For example, Giovanni Villani, a merchant-chronicler, pointed out that Florence's population of 90,000 in 1336–1338 required "about 4,000 oxen and calves, 60,000 mutton and sheep, 20,000 she-goats and he-goats, and 30,000 pigs."[5] This is not unrepresentative. Paris authorities reported that 269,256 animals had been slaughtered in 1293, and they itemized the count as follows: 188,522 sheep, 30,346 oxen, 19,604 calves, and 30,784 pigs.[6] Poultry and rabbits were generally not considered very desirable meats, and they were usually left to the lesser guilds. Thus, even the nature of the demand tended to favor the guilds.

The scarcity of the supply to keep up with this demand was related to the high costs associated with the fattening of stock. High demand and relatively low supply tended to generate inflated prices. Although there was a desire on the part of both church and state to maintain a "just price"[7] through secular and ecclesiastical legislation, the guilds' desire for profits and their ability on occasion to further restrict supply by inducing rural suppliers to withhold their stock tended to drive prices up. At the same time, communal officials needed to meet the rising costs of governmental operations and military ventures, a circumstance that frequently induced them to close their eyes to the rising meat prices while taking positive steps to increase tax revenues based on the sales of meat and meat products. For example, the Commune of Siena saw the revenue from the "gabelle," or tax on meats (*gabella carnium, gabella di macello*), increase from 500–600 lira in the late 1200s to 9,000–10,000 lira by the 1330s.[8] Another gabelle, the so-called gabelle of the beasts (*gabella bestiarum*, or *gabella grascie*) was levied in an attempt by the Sienese authorities to have their cake and eat it, too; this was a tax on animals slaughtered in the *contado* and on animals passing through or out of Sienese territory. This legislation also contained a provision requiring that one-fourth of all of the animals brought into or through Sienese lands be left in the hands of the communal authorities to be sold to provision the city.[9]

The revenue, or at least the potential for gathering significant amounts of tax monies, was very attractive, not only to the communes and their officials but also to the butchers themselves, who also saw possibilities beyond the collection of tax monies.[10] Once again, Siena provides the best documented example. From 1297–1312, butchers and, on several occasions, the guild itself subleased the *gabella carnium*.[11] The purchase of the right to lease the gabelle was not only a financial decision, but it was yet another way in which the members of the guild sought to evade governmental controls and prevent commune officials from effectively monitoring urban price regulations.[12]

Another communal policy that was frequently turned to the advantage of the butcher guilds was the desire of communal officials to limit pollution within the city. The authorities sought to limit pollution by restricting the number of places where butcher shops might be located. This type of restriction also had the effect of limiting, in some cases severely so, the number of butcher shops or retail sites. This provided the butchers, who owned the limited number of sites, with opportunities for price-fixing and limiting local competition. Some individuals leased out their interests to nonguild members while they concentrated on the more lucrative business of fattening animals for the market; in fact, in some towns the butchers no longer operated the butcher-shop sites (or the concessions) that they owned but rather leased them out to nonguild butchers or other individuals. Since these butcher-shop locations were so limited and the business so lucrative, individuals with surplus capital, who frequently had no connection with the trade, purchased these sites and ran them for a profit.

Perhaps the only place where the commune officials were able to maintain the actual intent of the laws they passed was in the area of sanitary laws. Once again, there was a conscious effort to require that butchers and meat sellers practice their trade in a manner that would not be injurious to the health of the city's inhabitants and that would leave the city's roads and waterways free of the by-products of the butchers' trade.

Food Supplies

The supply of grain and grain-fed livestock for the various urban populations was a persistent concern for communal officials. Population densities during this period were extremely high and, indeed, in some cases even surpassed modern population densities for the same areas. Pistoia had a population of about 44,000, of which about 10,000 lived in the city itself (about 49 persons per square kilometer, or about 0.386 square miles); Florence, in 1318, had a population of 116,200 in the city and 139,500 in its hinterland (about 65.5 persons per square kilometer), a total of 255,700. Although David Herlihy has argued convincingly that this population was declining in the century prior to the Black Death (1345–1350), the fact remains that this population was stretching, to its fullest extent, the capacity of the soil to produce plant and animal food—even after resorting to extensive land reclamation projects and the use of marginal land and highland areas for pasturage.[13] The pressure on the commune officials thus was real and not merely the result of political action.

The Ferrarese authorities were especially concerned about the status of the food supply and, in particular, that of the meat supply. One law in the Ferrarese Statutes of 1287 required officials of the commune and dependent towns to make lists of all of the livestock in the area that included the condition and location of each animal. Based on these lists, which were to be submitted to the podesta, sureties were to be given by the owners to insure that these animals would not be taken outside of Ferrarese jurisdiction. Owners could also be fined for leaving their herds untended, the assumption being that untended herds not only could suffer losses but could also damage crops.[14] The underlying cause for this concern was expressed in one of the rare prefaces to a Ferrarese law; it simply stated that the law was enacted "on behalf of the commune and for the evident utility of the commune of Ferrara, and so that a more bountiful supply of foodstuffs should be kept in the City of Ferrara and its District."[15] Other towns passed similar legislation designed to enable the local commune to maintain control over its supply of meat; this was especially true in those situations in which the livestock was taxed or the meat itself was subject to taxation.[16]

Part of the commune's concern was necessarily related to land use. It is
more expensive to raise meat for protein than to obtain protein from plant
sources. Furthermore, animals generally require large amounts of pastureland to sustain themselves. Pastureland, like any other arable land in this
period, was valuable, and commune officials were routinely faced with the
problem of deciding whether the land should be used for crop production
or pasturage.

Verona, for example, would not even allow animal owners to pasture
animals in leas or grainfields without the permission of the appropriate
communal authority.[17] Ferrara officials spelled out the rationale for their
concern very clearly in this statute: "We decree and ordain that, for the
conservation of the grains and of other foods which are planted throughout the territory, no one from the inhabited areas of Ferrara and its District is permitted to send his animals into the cultivated fields from the
Kalends of April to the Kalends of October."[18]

Bassano not only forbade its citizens and foreigners to pen or graze animals "unless there is a prior agreement with the officials of the commune"[19] but also auctioned off the right to graze as long as the actual
landholder was in agreement—or, presumably, was not using the land for
grazing.[20] However, in the next statute, the Bassanese officials required
that citizens holding flocks or herds record the number of their animals in
a book that was to be kept in the chancery under the podesta's care and, in
a later clause, limited the number of cattle that could be held by a single
individual to 240.[21] The presumption is that given the volume of legislation in the Bassanese Codes of 1259 and 1295 regarding losses or damage
incurred by the owners of grainfields, meadows, and vineyards, the city fathers were reacting to problems caused by the overgrazing of animals that
were being fattened for the retail trade, both within and outside Bassano's
borders.

The consumer demand for high-grade meat—beef, mutton, veal, pork,
and goat—undoubtedly enabled the butcher to take a fair profit for his
services. Unfortunately, there was apparently ample opportunity for the
dishonest to take advantage of the buyer. And the commune officials realized that they had a serious obligation to protect the consumer. Bassano
required its butchers to swear an oath that they would sell meat at a fair
weight and that they would not misrepresent the meat they sold.[22] Furthermore, butchers could only sell meat that they had obtained through
the commune's officials, and under the penalty of a substantial fine, they
were required to sell meat to anyone who asked to purchase it.[23] At the
same time, the statutes forbade anyone other than a butcher to sell fresh

meats, although nonbutchers were allowed to sell sausages and salted meats.[24]

The Bassano Statutes of 1295, which deal with the butchers' craft, represent a rather extensive expansion of the 1259 statutes and also reflect a certain amount of exasperation with the town's butchers, who had apparently found new ways to cheat the consumer. Butchers were specifically cautioned against putting their thumbs on the scale (to give a dishonest weight) and were warned against selling diseased meat, carrion, one type of meat for another, entrails, or animals killed by wild beasts. The podesta was compelled at the very beginning of his term of office to assemble the butchers in order to read the pertinent statutes to them. He was also to collect fifty-pound sureties from each butcher to insure compliance with the law and was supposed to investigate daily any complaints lodged against butchers. The butchers themselves were required to swear an oath to uphold these statutes and refrain from selling any meats not sealed by the commune officials and to obey all regulations regarding the manner in which meats were to be displayed for sale. In 1301, this statute was further amended to require that the butchers present "200 rams and castrated animals to the Lord Podesta at the beginning of May . . . so that they might be used in Bassano whenever they might be required by the Lord Podesta and the officials of the Commune." As if this were not enough, the butchers were required to keep these animals at their own expense until they were ordered to be turned over to the commune.[25]

Verona also enacted extensive legislation governing its butchers. They, too, were required to give "adequate surety" before they could "practice the butcher's art." Sureties were not only demanded from the butchers but from their apprentices and employees as well.[26] Some Veronese butchers were apparently less than honest with their customers, since the statutes specifically forbade them to sell rotten meat,[27] to misrepresent meat,[28] and to sell meat that they themselves had not raised.[29] A fairly extensive body of legislation also set prices for specific meats and meat by-products.[30] And finally, butchers were expected to sell to whomever came to them,[31] at a fair measure,[32] and they were not permitted to remove from their shops or conceal any of the meat entrusted to them.[33]

Piran was also not completely convinced of the honesty of its butchers and warned them against accepting stolen meat. In this case, however, the city fathers were careful to place these statutes with others dealing with similar, theft-related problems.[34]

The butcher's craft itself was closely regulated by the statutes of many towns to insure that the meat was distributed among the inhabitants in a fair, equitable, and reasonably sanitary manner. Ferrara, for example, cautioned its butchers to "state openly, whether the person who is buying wants them or not, that the meats are from this one or that one" and to sell those customers as much as they wished to buy.[35] Verona was concerned lest its butchers hoard their meat and specifically warned them not to hold meat back from buyers.[36] Furthermore, they were threatened with severe legal penalties in case "they should presume to carry off the aforesaid meats to their own homes or to someone else's, beyond those meats which were sufficient to feed themselves and their households for a single day, or to keep those meats concealed in chests or small compartments."[37] Not content merely to tell the butchers how to conduct their business, the town governments also told them where to conduct it. For example, in Ferrara, legislation outlined specifically where along the Po River butcher shops could be located.[38]

As has been discussed in Chapter 2,[39] there was a practical reason for locating the butcher shops in specific areas and quarters of the city. The slaughtering of animals resulted in large amounts of waste, leaving city officials with the problem of how to dispose of this waste in a sanitary manner. Butchers in cities such as Verona, Bassano, and Bologna simply dumped the by-products in various parts of their respective cities until this practice was forbidden by law; legislation in Bologna, put forth in 1288, required that the butchers take all waste products resulting from their craft outside of the city for disposal. Ferrarese officials required that the city's butcher shops be located along waterways and further required meat cutters to have an enclosed ditch alongside their shops into which the blood of animals was to be discarded.

The Leather Workers' Guilds

The economic success of the leather workers' guilds was closely tied to that of the butchers. Like the butchers, many of the tanners grew rich through their control of the trade. Often this accomplishment was achieved through a working arrangement with the butchers' guilds in regard to the prices of hides and skins. The nature of the trade, which was predisposed toward the production of high-priced, high-quality goods, enabled the tanners to exact large profits while supplying raw materials to other artisans, such as cordwainers, saddlers, and belt makers.

The difficulty facing the medieval commune concerning tanners was that the tanning process, which was complex and required the use of toxic chemicals, created serious pollution. The first stage of tanning involved cleaning and softening the pelts and removing hair and decaying meat.

The hides were passed through a series of vats containing slaked lime, which tended to "plum the skins" while preparing them for additional chemical processing. The hair and skin were then scraped away. Depending upon what the leather would later be used for—clothing, shoes, or purses—the hide was dipped in a cold solution prepared from chicken or pigeon carcasses or in a warm solution prepared from dog dung. This produced a chemical or bacterial reaction that removed the lime and albuminous material and left the skin pliable. The skin was once again scraped and then, depending upon the quality of leather desired, the skin was again washed or dipped in a mildly acidic concoction produced by fermenting bran. The hide was then scraped on the flesh side until the desired thinness was obtained.

Once the cleaning process had been completed, the leather had to be prepared for production by using one of three processes: (1) the oil process, or chamoising; (2) the mineral (alum) process, or tawing; and (3) the vegetable process, or tanning. These procedures were used to preserve the leather from decay.

Each of these processes involved chemicals. Chamoising required the use of oil, and tawing required the use of a salt-alum solution. Water-resistant qualities were added to the leather by tramping on it in shallow tubs containing a mixture of salt, alum, egg yolk, flour, and oil. The tanning process itself was based on the use of tannin, or tannic acid, which was derived from oak bark or sumac.

The actual tanning process, as was discussed in Chapter 2, produced large amounts of chemical wastes that were often dumped into the town's rivers, streams, and sewers. Certainly, it was a primary concern of the statute makers to prevent hazardous practices such as these, which would surely be detrimental to communal health.

Surprisingly enough, legislation referring to the tanners is very sparse. Even more interesting is the fact that the medieval municipal statutes are quite silent on the conduct of the leather workers, their trade, and their prices. The only matter about which the statutes indicate a clear concern is the disposal of waste products generated by that trade.

The Ferrarese statute makers, almost as an afterthought, appended a statute to the end of the Fourth Book of the Code of 1287 in an attempt to prohibit the leather workers from the unhealthy practice of disposing of animal by-products in the town's cesspool or in the Po River.[40] Clearly, the city fathers did not want the wastes generated by this craft dumped indiscriminately within the town's environs.

Bassano's legislators, too, were concerned about the waste-disposal practices of the leather workers. Not only did they limit where by-products could be dumped but Bassanese tanners were restricted as to where they could carry on their livelihood.

The River Adige was protected by Veronese law makers. Laws prohibiting the disposal of wastes into the river during the day but curiously allowed the practice at night "into running water."[41]

The products of the leather workers were necessary to the residents of the towns. Legislators in most northern Italian communes appeared to be concerned about the health and well-being of the residents of their communities and enacted legislation that was aimed at the protection of those residents. Concerning the consideration of the welfare of the towns downstream, one would hope that the elites believed that sunlight and the aerification of running water would cleanse the pollutants from the drinking water necessary for the livelihood of the downstream residents.

The Fisheries

In addition to meat, fish served as a major source of protein in the medieval diet. Generally speaking, fish was eaten more frequently than it is today because meat was rather expensive and few could afford it more than once a week. Fish was served fresh, dried, or salted. A large variety of fish was consumed throughout Europe and included such diverse varieties as salmon, cod, herring, mackerel, eels or lampreys, sardines, crabs, oysters, and mussels. To render these products salable, they had to be cleaned, dried, or salted; this process and the marketing of the fish were among the prime concerns of the town fathers.

The inland cities located on rivers, such as Bassano, Ferrara, and Verona, apparently had fish populations substantial enough to support a fish market and its related industries. Bassano's fish catch was small enough to warrant the commune's interest only in the marketplace, where price and weights and measures controls were imposed.[42] Fish seemingly played a more important part in the Ferrarese diet than it did for the Bassanese. The Ferrarese had established a fish market and insisted that fishermen[43] and merchants[44] alike bring their fish to this market for sale, especially during Lent. Fish was not under any circumstances to be removed from the city or its district by the Po fishermen or the merchants.[45] The only exceptions to this general rule were fish that could be sold by agreement to other towns, to personal friends, or to the owners of fishponds.[46] The supply of fish must have been a serious concern to the statute makers; they repeatedly warned merchants not to take fish out of the town and directed fishermen to bring their catch only to the town marketplace.[47] In addition, merchants selling salted fish were exempted from the direct salt tax since they were already paying a tax on the fish.[48] And furthermore, the statute makers provided clear instructions that anyone who sold fish could do so anywhere without any guild being able to obstruct them.[49] The provision of a stable supply of food for the Ferrarese populace was an obvious concern of the elites and was suitably reflected in their legislation.

The Veronese concern regarding the supply of fish and its sale within the city to Veronese residents was very similar to that of the statute makers of Ferrara; the supply was limited and had to be directed to the local citizens.[50] The Veronese were also concerned about maintaining the supply of fish from an environmental standpoint. Fishnets were limited in size, and the time of year in which fishing was allowed was restricted, as has been discussed in Chapter 2. These provisions were apparently strictly enforced, as guards were stationed to monitor the activities of the fishermen. The Veronese municipal officials, however, exercised a more complete control over their marketplace than their Bassanese or Ferrarese counterparts did. Fresh fish had to be sold in the marketplace[51] "in open dishes or trenchers" (although sardines could be sold in boxes);[52] fish could not be removed from the marketplace unless it had been labeled,[53] and it could not be taken home to the fishmonger's residence but rather had to be stored in the Palace of the Commune overnight.[54] The concern of the statute makers seems to have been motivated both by an interest in maintaining financial control over the market and by the desire to insure the freshness of the fish for the consumer.

This same concern for the safety and health of the commune's residents is reflected in the statute makers' concern that fishermen not dirty the marketplace with their refuse[55] or pollute the riverbank with the waste products of the fishing industry.[56]

Located on the Adriatic Sea, Piran perhaps maintained the most comprehensive control over its fishermen. Statutes required that fishermen pledge themselves each year to the commune; statutes also restricted the length of the fishing season, limited the sales of fish to the town marketplace, and set forth directives on the disposal of wastes that resulted from the preparation of fish for market.[57] A rudimentary environmental awareness appeared here, which was based on a strong measure of self-interest. The elites understood that there was a distinct relationship between the abuse of the environment through overfishing and future poor harvests.

Market and Land Resources

Similar concerns are again found in the legislation regarding the communes' supplies of grain and bread. The sales of bread and various grains were carefully monitored to insure that the markets were fair,[58] sales were adequately taxed and regulated,[59] and supplies were not sold beyond the communal borders.[60]

For our purposes, the manner in which the communes utilized their land resources is germane. If David Herlihy's data from Pistoia in 1244 are not atypical, then two factors emerge. First, nearly one-half of the commune's rural population was not settled on the commune's best lands but rather upon "steep, dry, and uncompromising slopes between 500 and 1,500 meters in altitude." This settlement pattern, not replicated in the same area today, was due to a number of factors such as the need for security, sanitation, and land easily cultivated with contemporary agricultural implements. The peasant population lived in many scattered small villages, where they worked small, noncontiguous, often unfertile plots of land without the assistance of oxen, fertilizers, or hired labor. The share-cropper-like conditions made for a kind of agriculture that was only barely removed from the most primitive forms of subsistence farming. Second, Herlihy has pointed out that the yield at harvesttime was anything but spectacular. He estimated that the break-even point for a peasant seeking to pay his land rent and to build equity was a harvest of ten seeds to one planted, or ten capacity measures of grain to each measure of seed sown. This yield figure was realistic for relatively good land located near the river bottoms, which was intensely farmed with the use of animals, fertilizers, and the best technologies known; unfortunately, this yield would not have been the general rule within the *contado*.[61]

Accordingly, the commune was faced with decisions about how to produce sufficient grains for its daily bread production, given its frequently marginal land, a declining agrarian population,[62] and a stable, if not increasing, urban population.

Spoleto, in a prefatory statement to a statute authorizing anyone "to come to sell and convey freely [that is, without tax] grain in the city," stated that the people who would be selling food in the city were granted this tax-free privilege "so that the city of Spoleto and its inhabitants should rejoice in an abundance of food supplies."[63] This appears to indicate that the town was having a problem obtaining food—a problem that was serious enough to warrant the town fathers forgoing a portion of their tax revenues to induce food provisioners to bring needed supplies to the city.

Piran handled the problem in a different way. The town quartermaster was obligated to utilize town revenues to purchase grain and other foodstuffs from anyone, foreigner or native, and to store the grains in the town storehouses. He was then required to sell that grain to bakers or anyone else at the price set by the podesta. The town had eight bakers, all of whom were required to buy from the quartermaster and render an accounting of their services to the commune upon demand. Furthermore, a rather stringent code of ethics was built into the law to compel the honesty of baker and quartermaster alike.[64]

The Piranese also recognized that there was a conflict of interest between its butchers and bakers. Meat was, and still is, a rather inefficient means of providing adequate protein in the diet of a population; that is, it takes a disproportionate amount of pastureland to produce one pound of meat. Consequently, meat was expensive and was eaten primarily by the more well-to-do classes. Bread products were produced more efficiently (that is, with a greater yield of food per acre) than meat and were therefore cheaper and more readily available to the poorer classes. The statute makers recognized this problem and limited the amount of precious arable land that could be used to pasture animals. For instance, in 1307, the Piranese statute makers declared that "no one can enter or keep more than ten *sapores* (or parcels) of the land belonging to the communes or to anyone else to pasture their animals. And they are obligated to pasture their animals on those lands for no more than four years."[65] The presumption here was that a given parcel of land could be used for four years for pasturage and then had to be returned to cultivation. There was also perhaps a bit of unconscious wisdom shown here as well—the land would be naturally fertilized over the four-year period by animal dung, and the rejuvenated soil could reasonably be expected to produce greater crop yields.

The statute makers of many communes took pains to expressly forbid the export of grain products, to limit the amount of flour that a baker might have on hand, to require that he provide an accounting for the grain products that he had been given, and to prevent hoarding.[66] The Veronese statute makers, like their counterparts in Piran, realized that the land had to be protected against overgrazing and that the crops themselves had to be protected against the deliberate or accidental invasion by herdsmen and their animals. Accordingly, Verona enacted legislation compelling both public officials and the responsible private officials or administrators of partnerships, companies, or similar private holdings to look to their duties and to the protection of the landed investment.[67] Subsequent statutes prohibited pasturage in meadows, vineyards, olive groves, and gardens without the permission of the owners[68] and also the permission of the *saltuarii* of the commune, who acted as semipolicemen in enforcing communal regulations.[69] Both the *saltuarii* and the castellans of the commune were required to report to the *massarius* (mace bearer) regarding their efforts to protect the lands under their jurisdiction and to indicate the amounts of the fines they had collected in enforcing the statute.[70] The remainder of this very extensive statute specified what fines were to be assessed against those who caused losses in the different types of agricultural holdings and against those who hoarded or otherwise diverted produce and outlined the procedures to insure official compliance with the statute.[71]

The general trend obvious in all of this land-related legislation is that the commune did not try to tell farmers or herdsmen how to cultivate, graze, or otherwise utilize the communal agricultural base. But in its desire to insure an adequate supply of cheap grains for all of its inhabitants, the commune utilized its power to prevent abuse, overgrazing, or loss to the annual grain, olive, grape, fruit, or vegetable harvests.

The Cloth Industries

Clothiers, flax workers, and cloth-makers of almost every description come under the scrutiny of the communes as well. The textile crafts rapidly developed from domestic occupations into highly organized industrial operations that included the professions of weaver, fuller, dyer, flax worker, and shearer. The products themselves led to considerable mercantile activity, the rise of new trade routes, and the holding of numerous cloth fairs throughout Europe.

Four types of fibers were used in textiles: (1) animal coats, especially the wool of sheep; (2) vegetable bast fibers, of which the most common was flax; (3) silk; and (4) vegetable seed-hairs, especially cotton.

From the environmental standpoint, wool, silk, and cotton products caused little concern, other than perhaps the disposal of the lye used in cleaning wool. Flax, however, was an extremely important concern since it was the most vital vegetable fiber in Europe until about 1300 and the source of the region's linen cloth.

In Europe, flax (especially *Linum usitatissimum*, which had to be resown annually) was raised and then harvested by cutting. Seed capsules were removed by hand or with combs, then the fibers in the stalk were separated from woody tissues through a fermentation process called retting. During retting, the stalks were immersed in sun-warmed water until the bark was loosened. Once the bark was removed, the product was taken out of the water and sun-dried. Next, the stalks were beaten to break up the woody tissues. The flax was then drawn through a comb of one sort or another to extract the fibers from the woody tissues and split up the fibers. The fibers were spun into yarn, and the yarn was eventually woven into cloth.

The retting process was of deep concern to the statute makers. Medieval cloth workers and manufacturers developed diverse methods of retting in order to utilize different water sources, and they used just about any supply of water available to them, including ditches, sewers, streams, and fountains. When they used the commune's drinking water or sewers, they came into conflict with communal authorities concerned over public health.

The cloth-finishing process also came under the purview of the communal authorities. Both woolen and linen cloth were washed after weaving, cleaned of extraneous matter, and either fulled or scoured (that is, the cloth was mildly washed and thickened). The purpose of these processes was to felt and thicken the cloth, mold the fibers closer together, and eliminate any holes created during the weaving process. A number of fulling agents were used in the cleaning and felting processes. During the cleaning process, soap, stale urine, lye-water, and various alkaline detergents, including lixivium (a form of lye) of plant ashes, or natron, were used. Fuller's Earth (a natural, finely divided, hydrated aluminum silicate) or plant juices, for example, from *Gypsophila struthium* L. and soapwort, were placed in a vat and the cloth was submerged in that solution for a period of time; then the cloth was removed, dried, and stamped by hand or by a mechanical means until the fibers were adequately felted. The fabric was again washed, rinsed, and beaten to further increase the adhesion of the constituent fibers. The cloth was then bleached by boiling in a lye of ashes or by exposing it to the fumes of burning sulfur. All of these procedures involved the use of chemical agents that frequently found their way into the communal waterways.[72]

Bassano and Verona both enacted predictable legislation enjoining the cloth guilds from washing wool and wool fell, or from soaking flax, in the town's waterways.[73] The guilds were also warned against storing unprocessed flax, ashes, old wood, or other chemicals within the town.[74] Ferrara simply forbade its residents to prepare flax within its jurisdiction and allowed its residents to keep only enough flax for a family's personal use; citizens were specifically warned against trying to sell flax and were threatened with fines and confiscation of the flax if they violated the statute.[75]

Conclusion

The communes did express some very definite environmental concerns through their craft legislation. The supply of food and water was of primary interest to the communes, and they therefore sought to protect that supply in several ways. First, they introduced a style of land-use management that attempted to strike a balance between the production of meat products and plant foods and that was geared toward preventing overgrazing and damage to agricultural lands. Second, they enacted legislation forbidding guilds to engage in practices that would pollute the communal water supply through the dumping of industrial chemicals or industrial by-products in places that would affect the health of residents. Third, they forbade craftsmen to pollute the city's environment with their waste products and industrial processes. Conservation practices were also exhibited through the communes' tightening of their control over food and land resources, their attempts to regulate an equitable distribution of food and water resources, and their condemnation of hoarding and other unfair or unequal trade practices.

6

The Medieval Urban Response
to the Environmental Crisis

Wealth in any commune came from a number of enterprises, including agriculture, commerce, real estate, manufacturing and processing, service industries, transportation, and construction. The European population growth, which tripled between 1000–1300, placed further demands upon agricultural productivity. Ever-larger cereal harvests of grain crops with increased protein content, first realized in manorial Europe due to insurance crops such as barley, rye, and oats, were one of the primary reasons for the rising birth rates, which then enhanced land values. The additional profitability of landholdings led to more intensive cultivation of existing farmlands and more widespread reclamation of "wastelands" through deforestation, diking, drainage, and irrigation projects.

This land hunger led, in turn, to a reorganization of landholding, land-tenure, and labor-use arrangements. The years prior to 1300 brought the decline of the manorial system and the erosion of the large estates held by the crown, the church, and the upper nobility and ushered in the virtual elimination of demesne farming by serf or dependent labor and the creation of more flexible tenancies based upon rents and sharecropping arrangements.[1]

These economic improvements in the management of land had social consequences as well. Surplus agricultural workers now found their way into the cities or the villages immediately outside of the cities, where they found employment in domestic craft, manufacturing, and industrial occupations, as well as in the merchant, fishing, and military fleets of the cities.[2]

The cities benefited heavily from their hinterlands. Food, fuel, labor, opportunities for safe investments, markets, and tax revenues all made life in the cities possible. The primary beneficiaries of these revenues were no longer the ecclesiastics or the imperial treasury but rather urban secular interests. Thus, a new relationship was emerging in the medieval northern and central Italian cities—one in which an ever-more-aggressive commercial element was reaching out farther into the countryside to invest its capital in agricultural lands, employ rural labor in both agricultural and industrial enterprises, and impose an ever-increasing burden on the rural environs to support urban institutions and political or military objectives. The urban communes were also able to impose their system of law upon the rural parishes and alter the entire quality of life in those parishes after their own image.

Environment, Climate, and Law

Legislation enacted by the urban elites between 1250 and 1700 reflected their ever-increasing concern with the agricultural resource base of the *contado*. Efforts were made through legislation to exploit, protect, and maintain the commune's ability to provide for itself. Although self-interest and a desire to be self-sufficient no doubt motivated the enactment of much of this protective environmental legislation, the fact remains that the urban elites possessed some clear knowledge of the relationship between protecting the environment and maintaining an adequate resource base for the food and craft industries. They understood the need to strike some sort of acceptable balance between the use and abuse of the environment.

As interest in the economic possibilities of the countryside increased between the twelfth and eighteenth centuries, investment in, and preoccupation with, the overseas trade decreased. Concurrent with the rising interest in the countryside, the productive capacity of the communes decreased, trade investments declined, and upper-class business initiative and commitment to trade slackened off.[3] The experience of Venice seems to indicate that declining interest in the overseas trade, although coincident with the rise of other European trading giants, was related to interest in the commercial exploitation of the countryside and to a newly kindled belief that politics was the responsibility of the upper classes. As the political situation in many northern and central Italian towns stabilized in the years after 1250 as a result of consolidation or outright political and military domination by larger towns, agricultural pursuits and animal husbandry prospered. With secure profits derived from agriculture, local entrepreneurs were able to maintain stable domestic economies balanced by foreign trade, a reliable supply of food, and the raw materials required by local craft and industrial operations.

The years after 1250 brought with them concerns as well as prosperity. The pressure on local resources increased dramatically because of larger populations and heavier demands from the growing urban industrial base. This situation was further complicated by a shrinkage in the resource base that was caused by environmental factors. There appears to have been a distinct relationship between the development of environmental legislation and the gradual deterioration in weather and related environmental conditions.

From an environmental standpoint, the period of the High Middle Ages (1000–1250) was characterized by such a benign climate that historians have labeled this time "the early medieval warm," or, more commonly, "the little optimum," to distinguish this rather brief period from "the big optimum" of prehistory. During this period, there was explosive and continuing population growth traceable to three primary factors: (1) food surplus resulting from agricultural and industrial innovations, (2) political stability arising out of the growing military and governmental institutions of the cities, and (3) relative freedom from plague and disease.

Because of agricultural innovations and a generally favorable climate, agricultural output increased after 1000, although it was outpaced by the rapidly growing rural and urban populations. The relationship between population and agricultural output was reflected in the price of grains, which showed marked inflation from 1201–1280, even when adjusted for debasement of the coinage. A partial explanation for the increasing price of food lies in the control of the towns by the elites controlling the grain trade. They took pains to insure their control of the grain supply through enactment of legislation controlling the pricing, acquisition, and distribution of food grains.

After 1286, grain prices began to moderate with the advent of long-distance trade in grains and with the increasingly effective intervention by communal officials in local grain markets. The communes were acting both to insure a steady, adequate supply of food, to prevent excessive fluctuations in local prices, and to eliminate the potential for civil disturbances arising from food shortages.[4] These prices continued to moderate until 1329 when famine, reminiscent of the Great Famine of 1315–1317, struck again; prices then rose steadily until the 1400s.

The impact of communal policies on the agricultural hinterland was extensive. The depressed prices paid by merchants afforded peasants a slimmer margin of profit, and as a result, many peasant families were forced to leave the land to find employment in the growing urban industries and crafts.

Declining profits from local agricultural production induced the elites to seek other sources of profit from the land. In the 1250s, urban industries needed increasing amounts of animal products, notably wool and hides, at the same time that the demand for meat increased. The growth in the numbers of butcher shops and animal-related crafts (as well as a concurrent growth in regulatory legislation) after the mid-thirteenth century was marked by a corresponding growth in the size and number of cattle, sheep, and goats due to protein-enriched crops such as oats, barley, and rye, which were frequently planted as safeguards against the occasional destruction of wheat crops arising from adverse weather or climatic conditions. These so-called insurance crops were often used for animal foraging purposes. They also had equally beneficial effects on humans when they were adopted into the medieval diet.

The larger size of the animal herds required an increasing amount of pastureland. This growing use of land resources for pasturage was reflected in a corresponding increase in the number and sophistication of local statutes dealing with land use for animals, the sale of the rights of pasturage on both private and communal lands, and the protection of crops and croplands from damage by animals. To increase the amount of pasturage in an area where arable land was limited sometimes necessitated a massive dislocation in the rural economy and population. Rural families, unable to compete successfully with long-distance grain merchants in local markets, were forced to leave the land either because their profits declined or they went bankrupt. As a result, local agricultural production declined dramatically in the years just before 1350, and as the land was converted to pasturage to support the herds whose products were in such demand by urban industry, environmental legislation was enacted at the behest of elites who often controlled both the rural areas and the urban economies. Nevertheless, in spite of the commune's ability to import large quantities of grain from foreign sources and control the distribution of that grain, prices began to rise.

The economic consequences of the decline of local agricultural output in northern and central Italy underscored climatic changes that had begun to be noticed in the late 1200s. Alpine glaciers that had steadily been retreating began to reverse their courses, and as a result, many upland meadows that had been used for several hundred years had to be abandoned.

The deterioration in climatic conditions and the cumulative impact of past environmental abuses proved to be disastrous to agriculture and food production in many areas of northern Italy. The year 1315 brought with it excessive rainfall and the first all-European famine in 250 years. Excessive rain, record increases in population, a heavy dependence upon wheat, and the overcultivation of marginal arable land escalated the onslaught of famine. Cold and rain washed away productive topsoil and reduced crop yields by blanching wheat, destroying seedlings, and permitting weeds to proliferate. In Italy, the rather limited agricultural resource base was farmed even more intensively. In spite of a relatively good harvest in 1315, wheat yields dropped disastrously in the Great Famine of 1315–1317, and in spite of elaborate methods of provisioning themselves, European cities and their hinterlands lost over one million people by 1325 to malnutrition and related diseases.[5]

In areas where animal husbandry was supplanting agriculture, a similar increase in land use was noted. This intensified land use was mirrored by a corresponding increase in municipal legislation relating to land, crop protection, and legal problems arising out of the multiple use of the land resource base. In other areas where agriculture had given way to herding activities, city officials and the elites entered into long-distance trade with regions as far away as the African coast to secure an adequate supply of grains for their populations. In addition, towns enacted legislation to protect what local crops were still being grown and to insure that the produce remained in the town's marketplace.

The crisis caused by climatic change and the decision to replace crop production with herding activities had a profound effect on the fabric of the Italian commune. Periodic famines tended to produce legislation in which concern for the food-producing land resource base became increasingly evident. The preservation and distribution of scarce food supplies became the theme of more and more chapters within municipal law codes.

Because the greater cost of the reduced supplies of food required increasingly larger shares of the household income of middle-class and poor families, there was correspondingly less disposable income available to spend on the output of urban industries. This, in turn, further depressed an economy already suffering from a loss of overseas trade revenues and induced the elites to enact legislation that had a distinctively protectionist tone regarding local agricultural output and markets.

The two classes most dependent on the land for sustenance and identification—the landed aristocracy and the peasantry—also suffered serious dislocation as a result of these environmental changes. Whereas the aristocracy was able to draw even higher rents and profits from its holdings and thereby avoid many of the economic problems arising from these crises, the plight of the peasant worsened. Peasants were being squeezed, on the one hand, by higher rents, fees, banalities, and demands on their time, and on the other hand, they were hampered by weather conditions that were destroying crops long before harvest and by crop yields that were declining past the point of profitable return. The situation was growing serious and threatened to upset the precarious balance of power within the commune. If the communal leadership was unable to retain control of the situation, civil disorder would result, and the commune's ability to maintain its rule would be seriously compromised. The situation in the northern Italian city of Bergamo can be used as an ideal case study to investigate all of these urgent conditions and needs.

Medieval Bergamo

Nestled in the southern foothills of the Alps, west of Venice, Padua, and Verona and north and east of Milan and Torino, Bergamo is one of the major population centers of the northern Italian region of Lombardy. Modern Bergamo is a reflection of its historic past. The medieval upper town, connected to the modern lower town by a cable railway, provides a fitting setting for its architecturally unique governmental, ecclesiastical, and private buildings. In the lower city, flourishing textile mills, engineering works, commercial enterprises, and industrial sites offer ample employment to the citizenry and a meaningful link to the town's historic mercantile and craft traditions.

Bergamo has long played an important regional role. Prior to its fall to conquering Roman legions in 196 B.C.E., the town served as an administrative and political center for the Gallic Orobi tribe. The Roman occupation brought with it the benefits of secure Roman economic and legal systems and the ancient world's best municipal administration and its comprehensive legal system.

With the breakup of the Western Roman Empire under the onslaught of the Germanic invasions in the fifth century, Bergamo, like so many of its sister cities on the Italian peninsula, suffered the destruction of its culture and municipal organizations and the looting of its treasures. Under Lombard rule (568–774 C.E.), the town's defenses and infrastructure were repaired to accommodate the increased economic, political, and military activity engendered by its function as the administrative seat of a Lombard duchy. With the fall of this duchy, a power vacuum in the towns was created that in time was filled by the only authority remaining—the bishop of the local diocese. The German kings were willing to support urban-based ecclesiastical authorities because of the increasing economic and military power of the towns and the unreliability of the rural counts.

However, the temporary balance of power attained by the imperial state was short lived. The economic and commercial resurgence of the Italian cities in the eleventh and twelfth centuries prompted the ever-increasing independence of the city from both imperial and papal power. Local aristocrats, whose military power was fueled by new wealth, shook off the restraints of the church at the local level and that of the emperor at the regional level, even engaging in intracity warfare. Other factions within the city itself, empowered by craft and industrial activities, began to organize themselves into political-military organizations called communes, created with the specific intent of resisting the power and intrusions of pope, emperor, and overlord alike. The communes, unique to Italy, focused power at the local level, and this led to the development of unique local administrative structures and activities, including the drafting of statute collections designed to meet specific local needs. Bergamo became an independent commune during the twelfth century, thus its history provides an excellent model for the growth of communal government.

With the onset of the fourteenth century, a process of consolidation along regional and dynastic lines under the leadership of local families or under the *signori* slowly began to emerge. This consolidation was forced both by the imperial-papal power struggle and the trading activities of the various cities. The political landscape of northern Italy would probably have resembled a patchwork quilt of regional families vying for local advantages had it not been for the success of the Ottoman Turks in the eastern Mediterranean. The intransigence of the Turkish refusal to trade with Venetian merchants forced those capitalists to seek profits in the Italian hinterland. In order to secure the political and military stability necessary for successful economic activity, the Venetian government was forced to expand its military power westward into the Italian hinterland and eastward along the Adriatic coastline. As a result, the Milanese Visconti rule over Bergamo was broken through war and was replaced by Venetian rule by 1429.

Between the early 1200s and the early 1700s, the Bergamese elites produced a remarkably stable legal tradition whose local essence was preserved and maintained in spite of repeated invasions and successive overlords. This tradition is reflected and preserved in the final codification of 1727, which forms the basis of the following discussions.

Market Locations

The marketplaces of Bergamo, as envisioned by the elites who produced the Bergamese Statutes of 1727,[6] were probably the most restrictive, nonmilitary environment within the city. These marketplaces, protected by the law, were not only economically and socially conceived, but they had physical dimensions grounded in the elites' perception of the town's quality of life.

Both from a political and humanitarian standpoint, an adequate supply of food was a key component of a town's livability. The famines and plagues of the fourteenth century, which produced massive labor shortages, had convinced local officials of the need to undertake a proactive role in the control of the food supply inside the city as well as outside.

Bergamese officials, certainly as early as 1331, acted to identify specific sites on which markets could be located. In the 1727 codification, custom and practice were enshrined in the law: The grain market and the market for legumes were located "in the new public square next to the Church of St. Michael de Arcu and adjacent to the Palace"[7] of the Count of Bergamo and they were to operate only on Tuesday, Thursday, and Saturday. Violations of these ordinances and illegal market operation were to be heavily fined. The official rationale for locating the market under the very eyes of the communal government was to insure "a more copious and a cheaper supply of legumes and food grains," to insure the public good, and to support the political advantage of the city fathers and the more distant Venetian overlords.[8]

Bergamese officials had a very specific, if unspoken and unofficial, reason for being very precise in their location and limitation of the sites in which markets could and could not be placed. Medieval marketplaces, unlike modern American malls, were not noted for their cleanliness or decorum. Rather, they abounded with rats, vermin, refuse, stench, animal wastes and by-products, dirt, and noise. Statute 1 of Collation 7 of the Bergamese Statutes of 1727 clearly identified a number of residential loci, or sites, in which markets were expressly prohibited. By focusing market activity in a few locations[9] that were close to the very center of the municipal government and by limiting business activities to every other day of the week, the elites kept the sheer volume of pollution, physical as well as sensory, within reasonable limits and facilitated the cleanup and trash removal under street-related legislation.[10]

Although the official reasons given for this legislation are certainly plausible and probably reflected the political agenda of the leadership, subsequent statutes spoke quietly of more compelling needs. For example, Statute 2 mandated that individual farmers, who presumably were not using the public market, sell their grain and legumes in front of their homes and nowhere else; the intent here was to prevent the development of a black market dealing in scarce commodities and to provide for the efficient taxation and regulation of these commodities.

The potential for food grain and legume scarcities and the need to prevent the disastrous effects of famine and plague were underscored in more than one-half of the two hundred statutes in this section of the code. To cite one example, Statute 3 specifically exempted seeds from regular taxation during the sowing season as long as the persons transporting them certified that they would be planted and that the amount transported did not exceed the needs of the farmers who sowed them. Clearly, the communal government was willing to forgo a significant amount of revenue to insure that food was produced and was likely to find its way into the Bergamese markets. This policy stands in stark contrast to the commune's willingness to tax or forbid the movement of other goods outside of the immediate jurisdiction of communal authorities. The food supply was limited, and the commune intended to insure its availability.

Food Supplies

The intent of Bergamese food-related legislation fell into four major categories: (1) the maintenance of an adequate, fairly priced supply of food for the town's population; (2) the protection of public confidence in the markets through effective oversight of the town's system of weights and measures; (3) the generation of sufficient revenues to pay for the cost of the operation of the markets and their bureaucracies; and (4) the regulation of the markets to insure that they remained as clean, sanitary, and sensitive to the environment as the technology and tastes of the era permitted.

Statutes 4 through 118 of Collation 7 created a system of bread-related price controls intended to insure that bread products reached the consumer at a price deemed to be fair and equitable regardless of the current economic conditions and the fluctuations of supply and demand. Bakers were licensed and regulated, carefully defined as a class, required to submit to statutory injunctions and to conduct their business in city-authorized marketplaces, and strictly forbidden to hoard bread or produce it at less than the community standards.[11] The desire to provide a sufficient supply of bread was so strong that the communal authorities themselves were directed under specific penalties "to keep a sufficient amount of bread in their own warehouses" to be distributed in emergencies.[12]

Millers, responsible for the conversion of raw grain into flour, were also strictly regulated to make certain that they would return a full measure of unadulterated, usable flour to the baker.[13] The legislation saddled millers with extremely heavy fines if they were found to have tampered with the grain in any way. The underlying premise is clear. Peace within the city depended upon a relatively content population. A major cause of civil un-rest was an inadequate, undependable, or contaminated food supply. Al-though the overall quality and quantity of the food supply was often de-pendent upon factors—economic, political, and climatic—over which the municipal authorities had little or no control, the Bergamese elites nonetheless acted in a decisive manner to protect the town's grain and legume supply. The bread markets were allowed to locate in only a few specific sites to control the noise, dust, traffic, insects, rodents, and poten-tial fire hazards associated with the bakers' ovens. The Bergamese elites regulated all market activities and required all mills to be located along flowing bodies of water. Lastly, the communal officials insisted that millers and their workers act responsibly to prevent the products and by-products of the mills from polluting the town's streets.[14]

Next to grains and legumes, the most important sources of protein in the medieval diet were meat and fish. The herding of animals, however, created special problems because, among other things, it required the di-version of relatively limited land and plant resources[15] to the production of an expensive product. Thus, once the decision had been made to divert these resources to meat production, it was incumbent upon the municipal authorities to regulate carefully the sale of meat and animal by-products.

The first concern of the Bergamese officials was to determine where to locate the meat markets. This was a purely environmental issue because of the large amount of waste and excrement, noxious smells, swarming in-sects, and problems of disposal and pollution inherent in the butchers' craft. These concerns, even in the medieval city, tended to outweigh other issues such as fraud, mislabeling, false weights and measures, and tax eva-sion.[16]

Statute 146 placed the responsibility for the operation of the meat mar-kets in the hands of the commune and its bureaucracy. The commune was required to purchase, at its own expense and "for the decorum, utility, and advantage of the City of Bergamo," a site or a building and to construct a portico with market stalls for the use of butchers. The commune was also required to meet the needs of residents living in the outlying quarters and neighborhoods through the purchase of specific sites located along flow-ing bodies of water. Finally, the legislation explicitly forbade the operation of butcher shops in the streets of the commune or anywhere else outside of the designated areas.[17] The commune, rather than any private individ-ual or corporation, assumed the responsibility for a problem that was clearly beyond the scope and regulatory ability of the private sector.

Butchers were required to operate their businesses under the terms of concessions auctioned off by the commune. These concessions prohibited butchers from plying their trade on city streets or outside their shops. They were even required to kill animals in their shops or just in front of them and nowhere else.[18] Butchers were required, in a manner akin to the regulated activities of bakers, to maintain a sufficient supply of meat that would be sold at a just weight and at a fair price to any customer who offered to buy it, although it is interesting to note that the Bergamese elites explicitly used this legislation to break the monopoly over meat production once held by the butchers' guild. The rationale for the elites' reaction is unclear: They could have been acting to preserve local market competition in order to keep meat prices low, or perhaps they were simply restricting the profit margin (and disposable income) of a class of potential rivals for political power within the city.[19]

The vending of fish also fell under the commune's regulatory authority. Fish markets were established at specific sites both inside and outside of the city walls to control taxes, prices,[20] and waste products and to insure that the resource base was not destroyed by overuse. Statute 167 directed the "Lords Judges of the Provisions" to pay particular attention "to which lakes or rivers the fish are taken from, that [the persons holding the fishing concession] observe the law of the city, and that private persons are not fishing." Statute 169 further directed these officials to examine all fish for sale to insure that they were properly prepared and were not on a protected species list. Communal officials thus extended legislative control beyond simply maintaining a clean environment. They wanted to protect a vital resource threatened by overuse and occasional abuse.

Thus, the environmental thrust of the fish and meat legislation is evident. Town officials sought to segregate the pollution associated with the operation of food-related crafts in specific and limited areas of the city. The purpose of these restrictions was to keep the environmental impact of the craft activity manageable, at a level the commune could afford to control. What materials could not be flushed away by the local waterways were to be removed by craft workers or communal workmen on the days when the markets were not operating. Furthermore, when the elites perceived that a necessary resource was threatened with destruction, they were not bashful about enacting strong legislation to protect it. The elites recognized environmental problems and created laws to deal with them.

Public Sanitation

The Bergamese concept of public sanitation would hardly be considered analogous with that of a modern sanitary engineer. Yet there was a common appreciation for a certain quality of life within the community that the municipal officials were charged with maintaining.

There is little written by medieval officials or urban residents about their expectations regarding the level of the quality of life within their towns. Scattered bits and pieces can be gleaned from contemporary personal, secular, religious, and medical writings. The actual beliefs of the city fathers, even in the light of the contemporary and classical environmental literature available to them, can best be derived from a consideration of their actions. The beautification projects in medieval cities, especially those of central and northern Italy, speak to the willingness of Renaissance magnates to commit vast sums of personal and public monies to the visual and aesthetic revitalization and adornment of their environs. This spirit was reflected on a functional level as well. The spirit and intent of the Bergamese elites has been captured in one of the briefest statutes in the 1727 statute collection. Statute 182 reads:

> No one can butcher a horse, a mare, or any animal on a road, or in a public square of the Commune of Bergamo, unless it is done right next to the wall of the City, the Quarters, or the Suburbs of Bergamo, so that the filth or disgusting waste does not contaminate [those areas], under a penalty of five Imperial pounds[21] for each offense, apportioned with half going to the Commune of Bergamo and the other half to the accuser or the person who makes the offense known.[22]

The Latin text of this statute contains two exceptionally strong terms, *putredo* (something putrid) and *abominatio* (an abomination).[23] These words were not chosen lightly by the statute makers, and they reflect deep emotional feelings about the impact that the butchering of these animals and the attendant pollution had on the streets, squares, and public areas of the city. The statute makers acted to distance themselves and their fellow citizens from the rotting, smelly, and unsanitary by-products of the butchers' craft.

Although the elites acknowledged that the butchering of animals was a necessity of urban life, they underscored the fact that the unsavory aspects of the trade had to be contained. The decision to permit the butchering to take place "right next to the wall of the City, Quarters, or the Suburbs of Bergamo" was consistent with contemporary practice and belief. For example, Statutes 193 and 194 regulated the activities of various professional groups, especially those working with leather and animal hide products[24] and required them to go outside the city walls to perform their washing and cleansing operations. The tolls that would normally be assessed against products passing through the city gates were not imposed as long as the craftsmen were honestly engaged in preparing those products for sale. Significantly, all of these processes involved the use of strong, often caustic and pungent, chemicals. The loss of revenue and the potential for fraud arising from the nonimposition of the tolls was considerable, but the desire to keep the residential and public areas of the city free from chemical and olfactory pollution obviously outweighed all other concerns. The location of butcher operations along walls with access to water and the requirement that chemical-intensive industrial and craft operations be performed along the Serio River were based upon a long-held belief. The trades produced *putredo* and *abominatio,* and running water solved the problem. Contemporary belief convinced the authorities that running water removed the offensive material from the immediate environs of the city and that the natural function of water ultimately removed the unsanitary material from the river and related waterways as well. They were simply unaware of the role of microorganisms in the breakdown of the pollutants.

Municipal officials were concerned with three principal types of waste: human, animal, and industrial. All three were complicated seasonally by storm runoff. The approach to all three was fairly consistent: Waste materials had to be contained and removed from the city.

In any of the northern Italian cities, containment was probably the easiest goal to accomplish. Most houses and businesses had pits, usually stone lined, on their properties to contain waste; but containers had finite capacities and eventually had to be emptied. In Bologna, a statute of 1288 placed the responsibility upon the private individual. In words that were remarkably similar to modern municipal legislation regarding septic systems, the Bolognese statute makers insisted that home owners control the outflow of sewage so that it did not flow onto the streets, walkways, waterways, or private property of neighbors.[25] But the problems of containment and enforcement were conditioned by human behavior. The same Bolognese code of 1288 contained a statute requiring butchers to refrain from dumping animal wastes into public streets; the butchers complied, but then proceeded to dump wastes in vacant fields. That practice was also banned by an exasperated city council that required butchers to remove waste materials to dumps located outside the walls.[26] Obviously, an ever-increasing population placed greater demands upon the butchers' ability to produce meat and dispose of related by-products. At the same time, this population increase severely limited the amount of open space within the town that could be used for cesspools and other sanitary uses.

The capacity of any private sector to handle the problem of waste removal was quickly exceeded, and municipal governments stepped in to assist. Some of the earliest techniques involved the digging of ditches and the excavating of those dating back to the Roman era. The ditches carried waste materials to communal cesspools or waterways located both inside and outside the walls. In some towns, these ditches were flushed out only when the rains came, whereas other towns, more fortunate, were able to divert streams and other sources of flowing water through them.

Another approach employed by town governments was the use of regulatory power to force businesses and industrial operations to locate within designated areas that had the benefit of running water or, at the very least, to restrict them to only a few areas so that municipal authorities could handle the problems of disposal efficiently.

Returning to the Bergamo case study again, the problem of human waste, both in public and residential areas, remained a serious concern even into the eighteenth century. The city fathers, no longer content with the disposal of wastes into open ditches along the streets and byways of the residential quarters and neighborhoods, enacted specific legislation designed to limit the noisome aspects of the problem. Statute 199 forbade the repair of old sewer outfalls and latrines that emptied onto the public streets and required their destruction as soon as they become unserviceable. Home owners were nevertheless permitted to construct stone latrines alongside their homes according to very rigid specifications that insured that wastes be contained or emptied into the communal sewer system through underground conduits.

Removal of sewage and storm runoff via underground sewers and drains had become a matter of public policy in Bergamo by 1727. Statutes 3 and 4 of Collation 8[27] of the 1727 code directed the officials responsible for the streets, the lords judges of the streets, to see to it that all sewers were buried under streets or roads, whether public or private, at the expense of those who benefited from them, and that drains or internal plumbing be enclosed within the walls of the private dwellings they served. The sewers and drains, on public and private property alike, had to be so constructed and contained that

> they are not impeded in any way with the result that [the effluvia] can go and be redirected through the [underground sewers of the] streets, roads, or byways; and [this should be done] so that the sewers do not in any way appear outside of the walls, and so that they do not carry anything putrid or fetid to or cause any [pollution] for the neighbors or any other persons,

under a penalty of 10 Imperial pounds and more at the discretion of the Lords Judges.[28]

Once again, communal officials acted to contain sewage and remove it from the public view for both sanitary and aesthetic reasons. An interesting aspect of this legislation is that it also sought to protect neighbors and the general public from the irresponsibility of property owners who did not obey the environmental laws.

Collation 8 also contains a number of statutes that required property owners to construct, repair, and maintain a number of sewers, drains, and ditches that were intended to remove sewage or storm runoff from various areas within Bergamo. This work, enforced by the communal authorities, was to be done at the expense of the named owners and those who "benefited" from the drainage. Failure to do so merited severe penalties. The rather innovative approach to paying for these improvements, namely, requiring those who benefited to pay for them, relieved the communal treasury of a rather substantial expense. It also insured that the communal government, that is, the elites, would receive public approval for improving the environmental quality of life within the community without increasing communal tolls or taxes.

Apparently, the Commune of Bergamo, like so many of its counterparts, had an age-old problem with its citizenry. Statute 196 implemented a general prohibition against public urination in the streets, under a penalty of 10 pounds, except in time of war when urination was permitted in areas away from the main streets. Bolognese statute makers in 1288 specifically informed citizens that they were not to urinate in the palaces or porticoes of the commune under the penalty of a heavy fine. Whether they were making a political statement or not, it is clear that municipal authorities were taking steps to improve the livability of their towns.

Public sanitation was another component of the elites' vision of an enhanced quality of life. Seeking to insure that the environment of their towns would be pleasant to eye and nose, they enacted strong legislation to enforce their vision and passed the cost along to those who would benefit most from the civic improvements.

Roads, Bridges, Waterways, and Fountains

From an environmental standpoint, the various elements of the urban infrastructure elicited different responses from the urban elites. On one level, each component of this infrastructure facilitated the economic, political, social, and cultural interaction of the human community; on another, the absence of these features prevented the physical interaction of the community within the environment of the town. Without a functional infrastructure there could not be an acceptable quality of life or, for that matter, a decent urban environment. It is within this latter context that the role of the elites in the maintenance and preservation of that infrastructure is considered.

The markets of Bergamo were the heart of the town's business life and economic activity, but the roads and bridges were its arteries. Crooked, narrow, and enclosed by surrounding buildings and structures, they nonetheless moved people, animals, and products through the town and its environs. The elites had a vested interest in keeping these arteries functional, free, and unclogged.

Statute 1 of Collation 8 of the 1727 statutes presented the elites' agenda for the streets and roads of the commune. "No person," began the statute, "of whatever status he might be, can or should take possession of, excavate, or damage the streets or the major roads of the City, Quarters, or the Suburbs adjacent to the City of Bergamo, or anywhere else."[29]

The public streets had become the resting place or disposal site for all-too-many pieces of private property—display tables, street stands, various kinds of wooden structures, privies, basins and vats of chemicals, crops, fodder, forges and ovens, animal and industrial wastes, and numerous other encumbrances. The lords judges of the streets were the communal officials charged with the responsibility, upon their sworn oath and a heavy penalty of 25 imperial pounds, of enforcing the law. They were required to check the streets at least three times a year, during the months of March, August, and December, to insure that they remained free, clean, and in good repair. Many of the regulations of Collation 7 directing the activities of the various businesses in Bergamo were alluded to, and the various tradespeople were warned under penalty not to block the streets with their display tables, fuller's perches,[30] ovens, stools, or any other structures. Private-property owners were also warned not to encroach upon the streets with their gatehouses or privies. Even those who were actually obeying communal law by cleaning the sewers and drainage ditches were reminded that they could not dump the excess gravel, earth, or debris onto the public roads, unless that material was needed as road fill. The exceptions to the rule are as interesting as the regulations themselves since they contain keys to an understanding of the elites' intentions. About the only tradesmen who were allowed special privileges were the shoemakers. Shoemakers living in Bergamo were allowed to display their wares on most Sundays and during Holy Week in the public square of the

Old Market and its environs; nonresident shoemakers could market their products in the same place on any day of the week as long as "they did not impede public access."

These last words were the key to the Bergamese road-related legislation. The environment of the roads had to be kept free and clear; the general public, merchants, and the business community had to have free access to the roadways at all times.

Roads, embankments, and bridges are not indestructible structures. The elements, time, and intensive use and abuse all combined to damage and restrict their use. The willingness of individuals to dump rubble and other wastes directly onto the roadways caused them to rise sometimes one foot or more over the years, requiring communal officials to "level" or "lower" them at considerable expense. In other places, the gravel, paving stones, and shaped stones of roads and bridges alike were removed for private building projects. Many statute collections in other Italian towns attest to the fact that human hands were as destructive to roads, bridges, and dikes as were the elements of nature. This wanton destruction of public property was an unmistakable, if often unheralded, result of the collapse of municipal and civil authority in the centuries following the breakup of the Western Roman Empire.

But the Bergamese elites did not have the luxury of contemplating their past. Accordingly, they expanded upon an existing legal concept, specifically, that those who derived the benefits from something should pay for it. The repair and the maintenance of the streets was a heavy expense that the Bergamese commune could not afford. However, the elites devised a policy that kept the roads and bridges open at the expense of those who derived the most benefit therefrom. Statutes 21 through 49 contain a common formula designed to accomplish this goal. Every road and street within the district of Bergamo was assigned to local communes, neighborhoods, and even to private individuals or corporations, who then had to assume the responsibility to repair and maintain them. Enforcement of the communal will was accomplished through the expedient of handing over the authority to compel the required work to a commission composed of the lords judges of the streets, a notary, and the chief workman,[31] who were to tour the streets to make certain that they were up to the standards enforced by the Bergamese laws. Even the salaries of the members of this commission were paid for by the individuals and entities benefiting from their services.

The communal waterways, dikes, and bridges also fell under the jurisdiction of the lords judges of the streets. The concept of "the waterways of the Commune of Bergamo" encompassed not only the natural waterways, such as rivers and streams, but also man-made structures such as sewers, ditches, and drains designed to bring water from natural waterways to private properties. Once again, the general rule was that those who benefited from the service provided by the waterway or the bridge paid for its upkeep. Because of the special needs arising from the use of water and water power, the communal elites enacted a policy that was not only based upon that designed for the operation of the streets but also further extended communal authority over individuals and corporate bodies residing in the district of Bergamo.

The need to draw water from the natural waterways and streambeds was acknowledged by the commune, but the cost of accomplishing that purpose was the responsibility of those deriving the benefit. The cost included not only the excavation of the watercourse but also the construction and maintenance of "bridges of stone or of well-ground squared stone," which should be "as wide as those streets and roads are" so that it be possible "to come and go through those streets on foot, horseback, or by wagon."[32] Recognizing the imperative for these man-made waterways, the communal authorities enacted a very comprehensive condemnation procedure that acted both to protect the value of private property and to recognize the wider communal needs. Certain locales, for example, such areas as moats and fortifications, were declared exempt from this policy because of communewide needs. However, individuals or corporations needing water for irrigation, livestock, or some similar purpose could initiate a legal proceeding, carefully monitored by the local communes and the Commune of Bergamo, in which the property needed for the project was handed over to the developer, who was then required to pay twice the property's market value to the owner as well as make the necessary construction improvements just described.[33]

Statutes 72 through 79 required the lords judges of the streets and the podesta himself, under severe personal penalties for failure,[34] to ensure that the waterways of the commune were cleared of debris, trees, and other encumbrances. Inspection, verification, and enforcement procedures were similar to those used to enforce street repair and maintenance, although there were more stringent and precise antipollution requirements imposed upon both the communal authorities and the local residents.

A new concern introduced into the legislation by the elites was the concept of pollution, in particular, water pollution. Statutes 72 through 95 cover in great detail the commune's concern for its water resource. The various waterways and their tributaries within the territory and jurisdiction of Bergamo were placed under the direct control of the podesta and the lords judges of the streets. Together with a team of four experienced

men and two chief workmen, these officials were responsible for the overall inspection, repair, and maintenance of the streambeds, ditches, and
plumbing through which water was drawn for irrigation, for the watering
of livestock, and for consumption by the residents of the city.[35]
Streambeds and ditches were to be kept clear to insure that water flowed
freely through them. The expertise of the chief workmen was utilized to
make certain that necessary repairs were made "in such a manner that pollution could not mingle with or enter into the waters, the measures of
land, or the water of the Lantrum [River]."[36] Thus, the responsibility of
the communal officials was to oversee the distribution and protection of
the town's waters and waterways and to operate the infrastructure that
brought water into the various neighborhoods and quarters of the city.[37]

Local communes and neighborhoods were given specific responsibility
for maintaining the fountains, laundries, watering troughs, plumbing, and
other water-related contrivances. To accomplish this, the consuls and residents of the various neighborhoods were required to appoint and pay the
salary of a custodian for each fountain and its appurtenances.[38] The responsibility of these custodians was to prevent the waters of the fountains,
watering troughs, and laundries from being polluted and to make certain
that the structures and their enclosures were protected from vandalism
and abuse. Public access to the fountains and other structures was guaranteed and anything, natural or man-made, that impeded public access was
forbidden.[39] Even more explicit was the ban on the pollution of the water
of those structures. Statute 85 stated that no one should empty any pollu-
tant into the enclosures or under the facades of the fountains of the City
or the Quarters of Bergamo, in the vicinities of those fountains, or in the
fountains themselves. No one should wash or deposit in any such water
sources any cloth, yarn, intestines, hides, meats, entrails, internal organs,
or anything else from which pollution might result, under a penalty of 25
imperial *soldi* for every offense.[40]

Hence, it is quite evident that communal officials understood the negative impact that industrial and human pollution, neglect, and intentional
abuse had upon the quality of Bergamo's water supplies. They acted deci-
sively to protect both the quality and the quantity of that water and its
distribution systems.

Fortifications

The municipal fortifications presented special problems. The statutes defined them as structures consisting of walls and moats. The walls had a
dual function, serving both as defenses and as delimiters of the city itself.

There was an unmistakable difference in the way in which municipal activities, governmental operations, cultural and social life, and communal fiscal policies were conducted inside compared to outside those walls. Citizenship and civic residency were extremely important qualifiers regarding the manner in which municipal law functioned. However, this function of the walls did not relate directly to the environment of the town.

The remaining component of the town fortifications, the moats, fell under the overall umbrella of water-related legislation. The effective operation of moats, which, generally speaking, were nothing more than wide water-filled ditches, depended upon a reliable source of water to keep them filled. Statutes 11 through 19 defined the communal policy regarding moat maintenance. The rector[41] was required to keep and maintain water in the moats at the expense of the Commune of Bergamo[42] and he and the elders of the commune were required to drain, clean, and repair them at least twice a year.[43] Subsequent statutes defined the construction, repair, and maintenance of other moats and defensive ditches in the territory and environs of Bergamo.

The water contained in the moats and ditches of the commune was not only a component of the town's defense but a resource as well. And the commune acted to protect this resource from abuse as effectively as it protected the waters within the walls. "Two men of good repute and reputation were chosen by the Elders of the Commune"[44] to protect and retain the water, to inspect the embankments and streambeds to prevent damage or unauthorized use of the water, and to initiate legal action against those who broke the law. Because the quantity of water was limited, only a few individuals were allowed to draw water from the moats for irrigation or livestock watering, and illegal use of the water or unauthorized cuts through the banks of the moats was expressly forbidden.[45] Damage to the moats, ditches, and waterways was to be repaired immediately at the expense of those who caused the damage, although the ultimate responsibility for the enforcement of this law fell to the podesta and other top officials.[46] The realization that water was a limited resource never deserted the statute makers, who set well-defined territorial limits outside of which new water-filled ditches could not be constructed.[47]

Despite the impact of the overlordship of the Venetian Republic upon the daily operations of the town government, the Bergamese elites were able to enact a comprehensive corpus of legislation that, among other concerns, protected the quality of life and the environment of their town. Such concerns as the municipal food supply and its sources, market, and distribution systems, the town's water intake and drainage systems, its air quality, and the maintenance of the town's infrastructure were all addressed in a comprehensive and orderly manner that assured the citizenry of the elites' willingness to make certain they would live as well as their technology and resources permitted. The Bergamese Statutes of 1727 stand as a mute witness to the determination of a small town to harness and protect the elements and resources of its environment for the betterment of the environment and the future citizens of Bergamo.

7

Conclusion: Things Left Undone

The efforts of northern Italian medieval cities to control and improve their environments were like "straws in the wind," in the sense that the phrase carries with it the notion of an event that acts as a portent, a precursor, an omen, or the harbinger of a future trend. The medieval tradition of environmental legislation did not represent a thoroughly integrated movement for the protection of the environment by the urban elites. Rather, it represented the efforts, often incomplete, sporadic, and sometimes misguided, of a class of literate, concerned political leaders at the local level attempting to provide for a respectable quality of life for the citizens of their community. They realized that their physical environment was a fragile, frequently damaged, but ultimately repairable milieu over which they exercised dominion, for better or for worse.

Although it might appear that we are representing these medieval urban leaders as environmental professionals, the fact remains that they left much undone as a result of their insufficient knowledge, technological deficiencies, or simple greed and self-interest.

For example, the law did not address the impact that rats, mice, and rodents had on the health and sanitation of the community. Community standards and concepts of cleanliness did not extend to the total elimination of the plant, food, and animal refuse upon and in which vermin subsisted. The medieval town, in spite of its urban character, remained an entity based upon an agrarian foundation that tended to encourage and sustain conditions in which this refuse was considered the norm. A direct result of this tolerance was an environment suited to the incubation and spread of infectious diseases that frequently decimated the urban populations. The transmission of the Black Death, which struck with such devastating effect after 1345, was facilitated by infected fleas carried by the black rats that thrived in the plant refuse so abundant in the cities.

In a similar vein, the failure of communal authorities to control the breeding sites of various insect populations contributed to the proliferation of swarms of annoying, disease-carrying flies and mosquitoes. More than just pests, they contributed to the contamination and destruction of food supplies and the spread of diseases such as malaria and encephalitis.

Most towns did not provide for the frequent and effective removal of refuse. Therefore, the accumulation of wastes within the towns not only supported the insect and rodent populations but provided for the incubation and spread of specific diseases generated by the decay of these materials.

Even the more effective methods of disposal resulted in damage to the environment. The removal of waste materials by flowing water inevitably led to downstream water pollution, and the removal of wastes into extramural dumps or cesspools resulted in the fouling of the local water table and the wells dependent upon it. Again, the result was contamination, contagion, and disease.

Disease resulted not only from practices that the medieval authorities themselves probably knew were unsanitary and unhealthy but also from activities that they never recognized as being potentially dangerous to citizens. For example, the statute makers produced a rather extensive body of legislation protecting the citizenry from frauds perpetrated by butchers in the labeling and weighing of meat and from the effects of unregulated disposal of the waste products of the butchers' trade. However, medieval technology and scientific knowledge did not afford the communal authorities more than the most rudimentary methods of meat preservation—salting, smoking, and drying—and the current knowledge and technology could not alert the authorities to the health-related implications of displaying meat products for sale on open tables exposed to the elements, insects, and bacteria. The net result was that the spread of food-related diseases was facilitated rather than curtailed by the legislation.

Even the air quality of the community suffered from the inadvertent impact of good-intentioned communal policies. The lack of efficient waste containers or an effective waste containment policy led the residents of Bergamo to burn much of their trash inside the walls of the city (in spite of a very real fire hazard) but to a greater extent to use the open dumps outside of the city. Construction practices sanctioned by communal authorities, and the limited and very expensive space within the city walls, tended to drive construction upward and over the streets, with the net result that the air within the city was even closer and more smog-filled than it might have been if the construction had been spread out over a larger suburban space. These practices, often born of ignorance and a lack of awareness of their eventual impact, tended to degrade the environment and sometimes offset the more environmentally friendly policies.

Unfortunately, the area over which the municipal elites failed to exercise comprehensive, effective control was the agricultural resource base and rural hinterlands that surrounded the towns. Although it is true that some elements of the elites and the wealthier merchants were tending to invest more of their surplus capital in rural areas as profits from overseas and foreign ventures declined and incurred greater risks, effective municipal political and legal control of the countryside did not keep pace.

In the case of Bergamo, for example, the conquest of the town and its hinterlands meant that the military forces of the Venetian Republic exercised effective control over the countryside. But the Bergamese elites attempted to regain some autonomous authority in the rural hinterlands by extending the authority of certain local officials, the lords judges of the streets, authorizing them to oversee the maintenance of roads and related infrastructure between the walled city, its suburbs, and a number of smaller, outlying dependencies. Within those areas of control, the local officials also acted to protect the local freshwater fisheries from overuse and abuse and to revamp amd maintain the irrigation systems that supported portions of the local agricultural resource base. But, as the experience of Viacenza under the Venetian Republic so clearly demonstrated, the small gains that local officials wrested from their overlords were few, limited in scope, and subject to frequent review and recall at the discretion of the Venetian leadership. Local authorities were in a constant struggle to maintain the prerogatives that they and their communal predecessors had wrested from ecclesiastical, imperial, and regional authorities; they were therefore not eager to enter into contests over political or economic turf that they could not win in the face of overwhelming political and military power. Such a loss would diminish the relatively fragile chains of authority that they exercised over their local populations. Hence, it appears that they would only confront more powerful overlords in those arenas where they anticipated a reasonable degree of success. Thus, although the elites may have wished to extend environmental controls into the hinterland, as the few attempts made by Bergamese officials seem to suggest, the fact is that they lacked political and military power to enforce any legislation applying to the hinterland. As a result, abuses such as overgrazing, erosion, deforestation, destruction of wildlife, and land and water pollution continued largely unabated in the rural hinterlands.

In spite of occasional failures, however, the medieval elites did accomplish a great deal in terms of preserving and enhancing the environment. The communal authorities of medieval Bergamo were among the first urban leaders to recognize that they had a communitywide responsibility to maintain and improve the environment and that they had the power and the authority to develop and implement an environmental policy. Most important, they acted to make changes within the limits of their resources and the prevailing technology. Within the constraints of their era and technology, these leaders developed one of the earliest comprehensive municipal environmental policies intended to improve the urban quality of life.

The importance of their efforts led to the transmission of legal knowledge, concepts, and techniques across the face of Europe, through England, and over to the New World. This new information was accompanied by concern for the environment and the notion that community environmental standards could be enhanced through the imposition of municipal law and policies. Hence, in many ways, the Bergamese elites and their peers in other Italian cities were the prototypical exemplars for modern and more efficient methodologies based upon the scientific advances of the recent past. And, so it is that the medieval urban environmental legislative initiatives, which were once merely straws in the wind, have become the cornerstone of the modern environmental movement.

Notes

Chapter One

1. Paul M. Hohenberg and Lynn Hollen Lees, *The Making of Urban Europe, 1000–1950* (Cambridge, Mass., 1985), p. 19.

2. Max Weber, "Class, Status, Party," in *From Max Weber's Essays in Sociology,* ed. and trans. H. H. Gerth and C. Wright Mills (New York, 1946), p. 180.

3. Ibid., p. 45.

4. Also frequently referred to as the *societas popoli* in some texts; members of the *popolo* were often referred to individually as *popolani.*

5. Vatro Murvar, "Occidental Versus Oriental City," *Social Forces* 44 (3) (March 1966), pp. 384ff.

6. Ibid., p. 45.

7. Gino Luzzatto, *An Economic History of Italy from the Fall of the Roman Empire to the Beginning of the Sixteenth Century* (New York, 1961), p. 70.

8. *Robert-Henri Bautier, The Economic Development of Medieval Europe* (London, 1971), p. 106; Carlo M. Cipolla, *Before the Industrial Revolution: European Society and Economy, 1000–1700* (New York, 1976), p. 143 and n. 4.

9. David Herlihy, *Pisa in the Early Renaissance: A Study of Urban Growth* (New Haven, 1958), pp. 176ff, and *Medieval and Renaissance Pistoia: The Social History of an Italian Town, 1200–1430* (New Haven, 1967), pp. 176–187.

10. Duane J. Osheim, *An Italian Lordship: The Bishopric of Lucca in the Late Middle Ages* (Los Angeles, 1977), pp. 2ff.

11. The *capitano del popolo* was the chief executive officer of the *popolo* and tended to be a military leader as well.

12. George Orwell, *Animal Farm* (New York, 1946), pp. 28, 148.

13. John Kenneth Hyde, *Society and Politics in Medieval Italy: The Evolution of Civil Life, 1000–1350* (New York, 1973), pp. 114–115.

14. Councillors usually had to be at least twenty-five years of age.

15. William H. Bowsky, *A Medieval Italian Commune: Siena Under the Nine, 1287–1355* (Berkeley, 1981), p. 87.

16. Bowsky, examining the data for the Commune of Siena between 1287 and 1355, has concluded that at least half of the councillors were Noveschi, or members of the Sienese elites; see Bowsky, *Medieval Italian Commune,* pp. 85–87. Herlihy reported similar statistics for Pistoia in Herlihy, *Pistoia,* p. 219. Indeed, Hyde, *Society and Politics,* p. 115, reported that membership frequently became hereditary.

17. Alexander Lisini, ed., *Il costituto del comune di Siena rigolarizzato nel MCCCIX–MCCCX*, 2 vols. (Siena, 1903), p. 519, and William M. Bowsky, *The Finance of the Commune of Siena, 1287–1355* (Oxford, 1970), pp. 48ff.

18. Notaries were individuals able to read and write who were employed as secretaries to write the minutes of deliberations and to perform minor legal tasks.

19. Bowsky, *Medieval Italian Commune*, pp. 87ff.

20. Bowsky, *The Finance of the Commune of Siena, 1287–1335* (Oxford, 1970), p. 264.

21. Bowsky, *Medieval Italian Commune*, p. 94.

22. Ibid., pp. 96–97.

23. Lauro Martines, *Power and Imagination: City–States in Renaissance Italy* (New York, 1979), p. 149.

24. Martines has pointed out that with the membership in these councils set at 600–700 and the terms of office at four months, eligible citizens would have the opportunity to sit on the Greater Council at least once every sixteen months (Martines, *Power and Imagination*, pp. 148–149).

25. A careful distinction must be made between the Lesser Council and an ad hoc committee that had very specific and limited functions and that was actually appointed by and responsible to the Lesser Council through the latter's ability to control the agenda and appointments to the Greater Council.

26. Martines, *Power and Imagination*, pp. 155–156.

27. These were officials charged with the enforcement of the statutes.

28. Gina Fasoli and Pietro Sella, introduction to *Statuti di Bologna dell'anno 1288*, 2 vols. (Vatican City, 1937).

29. Bowsky, *Medieval Italian Commune*, p. 124.

30. This was the court of the ruling council of Siena; see William M. Bowsky, "Medieval Citizenship: The Individual and the State in the Commune of Siena, 1287–1355," *Studies in Medieval and Renaissance History* 4 (1967), p. 225.

31. Bowsky, *Medieval Italian Commune*, pp. 106–107 n. 48.

Chapter Two

1. Plato, *Timaeus, Critias, Ceitophon, Menexenus, Epistles*, trans. R. G. Bury (Cambridge, Mass., 1952), 27–33C; 69B ff.

2. Aristotle, *Politica*, trans. Benjamin Jowett (Oxford, 1946) in vol. 10, W. D. Ross, ed., *The Works of Aristotle Translated into English* (New York, 1959), I.1.; I.v.; I.8.

3. Perhaps the best available source dealing with the intellectual basis for the environmental movement from its origins is Clarence J. Glacken, *Traces on the Rhodian Shore: Nature and Culture in Western Thought from Ancient Times to the End of the Eighteenth Century* (Berkeley, 1976).

4. Marcus Tullius Cicero, *De natura deorum. Academica*, trans. H. Rackman (Cambridge, Mass., 1951), II, 52–53.

5. Pliny, *Natural History*, trans. H. Rackman (Cambridge, Mass., 1938), II, 63.

6. Ibid., VII, 1; XVII, 3, 35–36.

7. See Michael Rostovtzeff's discussion of the Tebtunis Papyri 703 in his *The Social and Economic History of the Hellenistic World*, 3 vols. (Oxford, 1941), vol. 3, pp. 66–102.

8. Ibid., vol. 1, p. 316.

9. Strabo, *The Geography of Strabo*, trans. H. C. Hamilton and W. Falconer (London, 1854–1856), XVII, i, 3.

10. See *Asclepius* I, 6a; in Hermes Trismegistus, *Hermetica. The Ancient Greek and Latin Writings Which Contain Religious or Philosophic Teachings Ascribed to Hermes Trismegistus*, ed. and trans. Walter Scott (Oxford, 1924), vol. 1.

11. The notion of humanity as the "steward" of its environment was a concept originating in classical thought that passed into the Christian world despite the "otherworldly focus" of some Christian thinkers who followed the theology of St. Augustine.

12. It must be acknowledged here that although some schools of Judaism taught that there was a life after death, others did not; and the Hebrew Bible is not especially clear on the matter. Christian theologians, however, enshrined this belief in their theology and worldview.

13. "In the beginning God created the heavens and the earth: the earth was waste and void; darkness covered the abyss, and the spirit of God was stirring above the waters" (Gen. 1:1–2).

14. Gen. 2:15.

15. "For thus says the Lord, the creator of the heavens, who is God, the designer and maker of the earth who established it, not creating it to be a waste, but designing it to be lived in (Isa. 45:18); "You have made him (Man) little less than the angels, and crowned him with glory and honor. You have given him rule over the works of your hands, putting all things under his feet" (Ps. 8:5, 6); "Heaven is the heaven of the Lord, but the earth He has given to the children of men" (Ps. 115:16).

16. Ps. 8:6 continues, "Thou hast put all things under his feet . . . sheep, oxen, the beasts of the field, and the life in the sea."

17. This image of God being accompanied by a competent assistant who carries out his design is found in the person of Wisdom in Prov. 10:22–31.

18. "For since the creation of the world his invisible attributes are clearly seen—his everlasting power also and divinity—being understood through the things that are made. And so they are not without excuse, seeing that, although they knew God, they did not glorify him as God or give thanks, but became vain in their reasonings, and their senseless minds have been darkened. For while professing to be wise, they have become fools, and they have changed the glory of the incorruptible God for an image made like to corruptible man and to birds and the four-footed beasts and creeping things" Rom. 1:20–23.

19. 1 Cor. 3:9.

20. 1 Tim. 4:4.

21. Rom. 8:19.

22. Origen, *Contra Celsum,* trans. Henry Chadwick (Cambridge, 1953), IV, 74.

23. Ibid., 78.

24. Augustine, *Concerning the City of God Against the Pagans,* trans. Henry Bettenson (Bungay, Suffolk, 1986), XI.23, pp. 454ff.

25. Ibid., XI.4.

26. Augustine, "Contra epistolam Manichaei quam vocant Fundamenti liber unus," in *Oeuvres Complètes de St. Augustin,* French and Latin text. Trans. into French and annotated by Péronne, Vincent, Écalle, Carpentier, and Barreau (Paris: Librairie de Louis Vivès, 1872–1878), 34 vols., vol. 5, p. 476.

27. Philo (Philo Judaeus), "On the Account of the World's Creation Given by Moses," *Philo,* vol. 1, trans. G. H. Whitaker (New York, 1929), p. 88.

28. "De natura locorum," tr. II, chap. 4 in Albert the Great (Albertus Magnus), *Beati Alberti Magni, Ratisbonensis Episcopi, Ordinis Praedicatorum, opera quae hactenus haberi potuerunt. . . . Studi et labore, R.A.P. F. Petri Jammy . . .* (Luguni, 1651), vol. 5, pp. 282–283.

29. Thomas Aquinas, *On the Truth of the Catholic Faith. Summa Contra Gentiles, Book Two: Creation,* trans. James P. Anderson (Garden City, N.Y., 1955–1956), chap. 1, par. 6: chap. 2, par. 1; chap. 24, par. 4–6; and chap. 26, par. 6.

30. This doctrine is consistent with Gen. 1:3 and with Ps. 8 and 104; see also Thomas Aquinas, *Summa Theologica,* trans. by the Fathers of the English Dominican Province (London, 1947), pt. 1 q. 65, art. 2.

31. Ibid., pt. 1 q. 69, art. 2.

32. Thomas Aquinas, *Summa Theologica,* pt. 1 q. 102, art. 2–3.

33. Ibid., pt. 1 q. 96, art. 1.

34. Thomas Aquinas, *On the Truth of the Catholic Faith. Summa Contra Gentiles. Book Three: Providence Part 1,* trans. Vernon J. Bourke (Garden City, N.Y., 1955–1956), pt. 1, chap. 22, par. 3.

35. Aristotle, *Politica,* VII, 7; *Physica,* VII, 3, 246b; *On the Length and Shortness of Life,* I 7–10, 465a; Vegetius =Vegetius Renatus, Flavius, *Epitoma rei militaris,* ed. and trans. Leo F. Stelton (New York, 1990), hereafter *De re militari.* VII, 2; and Vitruvius, Pollio, *De Architectura* (On architecture), ed. and trans. Frank Granger (Cambridge, Mass., 1931–1934), bk. 1, chap. 4.

36. Thomas Aquinas, *On Kingship: To the King of Cyprus,* trans. Gerald B. Phelan (Toronto, 1949), p. 100.

37. Ibid., 124.

38. Ibid., 124; see also Vegetius, *De re militari,* I, 2.

39. Aristotle, *Politica,* VII, 7, 1327b, 23–32.

40. Vitruvius, *On Architecture,* I, 4.

41. Thomas Aquinas, *On Kingship,* 126, 128–129.

42. Georgius Agricola, *De re metallica,* trans. Herbert C. Grover and Lou H. Hoover (New York, 1912), p. 8.

43. Ferrara, *Statutes* (1287) II:ccxcix.

44. Bologna, *Statutes* (1250) VII:cxii, cxxiii, cxxviii.

45. Ferrara, *Statutes* (1287) IV:lxxvii.

46. The entire process is described in Charles Singer et al., *A History of Technology, vol. 2, The Mediterranean Civilization and the Middle Ages, c. 700 B.C to c. A.D. 1500* (New York, 1956), pp. 152ff.

47. Ferrara, *Statutes* (1287) IV:lxxvii.

48. Bassano, *Statutes* (1295) II:xliii.

49. Ibid., xxiii.

50. Verona, *Statutes* (1276) IV:clxxviii.

51. Ibid., clxxix.

52. Ibid.

53. Ibid., ccxi.

54. Verona, *Statutes* (1276) IV:lxxxvii, lxxxviii, xc, and xcii.

55. Ibid., lxxxvi.

56. Ibid., lxxxviii.

57. Ferrara, Statutes (1287) IV:lxxvi.

58. Piran, Statutes (1307) X:i.

59. Ibid., ii.

60. Ibid., iii.

61. Ibid., iv, v.

62. Ibid., vi.

63. Ibid., vii.

64. Ibid., vii, viii.

65. Piran, *Statutes* (1307), X:ix.

66. Ibid., x.

67. Retting is the process whereby seed capsules are removed and the fibers in the stalk are separated from woody tissues through fermentation.

68. Bologna, *Statutes* (1250) I:xxvi; VII:cxxviii; VIII:xcvii.

Chapter Three

1. The Greek sacred roads, such as those that linked Sparta and Anyklae, Athens and Eleusis, and the various cities to Delphi, were "rut" roads in which ruts were deliberately dug out, polished, and leveled to provide an easy passage for wheeled vehicles.

2. The Persian Royal Road was a "track system" designed to provide an improved messenger service as part of the effort to bind the far-flung empire together. Cyrus (circa 600–530 B.C.E.) had his engineers determine the distance that a horseman could travel in a day, and he ordered that stations with fresh horses, grooms, and lodgings be established one day's journey apart. But the road itself remained a barely improved track with stretches that were impassable to wheeled traffic.

3. It was not paved until 295 B.C.E.

4. Charles Singer et al., *History of Technology*, vol. 2, p. 500.

5. Statius, *Silvae*, IV, iii, 40–48 (Loeb Classical Library, 1921, vol. 10, pp. 212ff).

6. For example, there were several under Augustus.

7. These road-building contracts were frequently sought after because they were ready sources of graft.

8. These boards were first appointed by Augustus in 22 B.C.E.

9. For example, M. Fonteius, while praetor of Gallia Narbonensis, levied a tax on wine for the repair of local roads (*portorium vini*, Cic. *pro Font.* 5).

10. William Smith, William Wayte, and G. E. Marindin, *A Dictionary of Greek and Roman Antiquities*, 3d ed., 2 vols. (London, 1891), vol. 2, pp. 949–950.

11. *Digesta Iustiniani*, 43, 10, 3.

12. See, for example, the municipal law quoted by Mommsen, *Staatsrecht*, ii, pp. 505ff., as noted in Smith et al., vol. 2, p. 950.

13. J. J. Jusserand and Lucy Toulmen Smith, *English Wayfaring Life in the Middle Ages (XIVth Century)*, 3d ed. (Williamsburg, Mass., 1974), pp. 35ff.

14. Ibid., p. 38.

15. Ibid., pp. 38–39; Smith, Wayte, and Marindin, *Antiquities*, vol. 2, p. 525.

16. Ibid., pp. 41ff.

17. Streets were usually no more than sixteen feet wide, except for the main streets, which were usually more than twenty-three feet wide.

18. Pliny, *Natural Science*, XXXVI, xxiv, 104.

19. Lanes were to be eight feet wide, side streets twelve feet, secondary thoroughfares twenty feet, and first-class roadways forty feet.

20. The *cloaca maxima* of Rome was built about 500 B.C.E. for the purpose of providing adequate drainage for the area around the Forum, and it measured fourteen feet in height and eleven feet in width. Three other streams that were the natural drainage system for the area around Rome were channelized, paved, and turned into sewers by Roman engineers in a manner reminiscent of some modern American urban engineering projects.

21. See F. W. Robbins, *The Story of the Land and the Candle* (London, 1939).

22. They were similar to the law codes of the Holy Roman Imperial cities of Gottingen in 1330 and Mechlin in 1348.

23. This inference must be made given the widespread municipal legislation regarding pigs and their control. Only in rare instances does one note laws requiring pigs to be penned.

24. See Nuremburg Code (1490); B. Heil, *Die deutschen Stadte und Burgen im Mittelalter* (Leipzig, 1921), pp. 104–107.

25. This matter will be discussed further on in greater detail. However, this situation did have a practical solution as well. Shoemakers were required to make shoes that were heavy, high, and thickly soled.

26. "In the days of Alexander Neckam (1157–1217), the streets of Paris were in disrepair and full of mud" (Smith, Wayte, and marindin, *Antiquities,* vol. 2, p. 532).

27. Ibid., p. 532.

28. Joseph R. Strayer and Dana C. Munro, *The Middle Ages, 395–1500,* 4th ed. (New York, 1959), p. 405.

29. Bassano, *Statutes* (1259) II:xxxvii; *Statutes* (1295) II:xlix; Ferrara, *Statutes* (1287) V:xxix, xxx.

30. Bassano, *Statutes* (1259) II:lxx; Statutes (1295) II:xli.

31. Ibid., lxxiii.

32. Bassano, *Statutes* (1259) IV:lxxx, xl.

33. Ibid., cxxii.

34. These were injunctions against pack animals, Bassano, *Statutes* (1259) II:xxxix and against pigs, Ibid., III:vi.

35. Ibid., IV:lxxxvi.

36. Verona, *Statutes* (1276) IV:cxxxi.

37. Ibid., ccxii.

38. Ibid., ccxix, ccxx.

39. See Orvieto, *Charter* (1334) LXVII; Spoleto, *Constitutum* (1296) XLIX.

40. Spoleto, *Constitutum* (1296) II:vi.

41. See further in this text for many examples of medieval legislation; however, modern writers are equally concerned. Martin V. Melosi, in *Garbage in the Cities: Refuse, Reform, and the Environment, 1880–1980* (College Station, Tex., 1981), details ancient and medieval attempts to deal with refuse disposal in his first chapter and then proceeds to provide a historical perspective on the rising interest in refuse removal in the nineteenth and twentieth centuries. See also George A. Rosen, *A History of Public Health* (New York, 1958).

42. Books dealing with social customs frequently cite this as the reason why men in the company of women would walk on the curb side of the street during the Middle Ages. Presumably, it was considered better form for the man to receive the full benefits of whatever might descend from the skies or the upper stories.

43. Bassano, *Statutes* (1259) II:lxx; *Statutes* (1295) II:xliii; Ferrara, *Statutes* (1276) I:clxxii, clxxxix; Bologna, *Statutes* (1288) X:ii; Piran, *Statutes* (1307) III:x.

44. Bassano, *Statutes* (1295) II:xli; of course, it could be that this law was amended at the request of the podesta, who did not wish these materials to be accumulated in front of the town's citadel.

45. Piran, *Statutes* (1307) IX:xlvi, xlvii.

46. Bassano, *Statutes* (1295) II:xli.

47. Bologna, *Statutes* (1288) X:vi, x.

48. See, for example, Bassano, *Statutes* (1295) II:xliii, xliv, xlix; Ferrara, *Statutes* (1276) IV:lxxv; and Bologna, *Statutes* (1288) X:vii, viii.

49. Bassano, *Statutes* (1295) II:xlii.

50. Ibid., III:xii.

51. Spoleto, *Statutes* (1296) I:lxxi.

52. Spoleto, *Breve* (1296) XXV, LXI; *Constitutum* I:xlix.

53. See, for example, Verona, *Statutes* (1276) IV:clxxii, clxxx, clxxxvii.

54. Ferrara, *Statutes* (1287) V:xxi.

55. Verona, *Statutes* (1276) IV:clxxxvii; see also Verona, *Statutes* (1276) IV:clxxxviii, clxxxix, cxc; Spoleto, *Constitutum* (1296) I:xlix; *Statutum* (1296) XXI.

56. These situations occurred only in those areas when the question of who actually owned the land was unclear or where special circumstances warranted communal assistance, i.e., where the commune might have designated a roadway to be used by those carrying construction materials or straw (Ferrara, *Statutes* (1287) V:xlvi; see also V:lxii).

57. See Verona, *Statutes* (1276) IV:clxxxvii.

58. The raising and leveling of these roads was often necessitated by the fact that years of throwing garbage and other refuse out into the streets raised the roadbed level above the level of the surrounding properties. When the sewage or normal drainage from the streets into the nearby properties became serious enough, the city fathers would be petitioned to have the road surfaces removed, graded, and resurfaced with gravel or stones. See Verona, *Statutes* (1276) IIII:cxcii, cxciii; Piran, *Statutes* (1307) I:xiii, xiv; Bassano, *Statutes* (1295) III:xii; IV:xxxv; Orvieto, *Statutes* (1334) I:lxiv, lxxiv; Ferrara, *Statutes* (1287) V:xvi, xxxiv, xxxvii, lv, cxiii, cxlii, cxliii, cxliv, cxlv, cxlviii, cxlix, clii, clvi, clxiv, clxviii, clxxxii, cxcii.

59. Verona, *Statutes* (1276) IV:cxciv; Ferrara, *Statutes* (1287) V:xxxvi, xlvi.

60. Spoleto, *Constitutum* (1296) I:i; II:ii; Verona, *Statutes* (1287) V:xxi; Ferrara, *Statutes* (1287) V:li, lii, lxii.

61. Bassano, *Statutes* (1259) II:lxxv.

62. Ibid., 1.

63. Ferrara, *Statutes* (1287) V:xvi; also V:lv, lxiii, cxxv.

64. Ibid., lxxv, lxxvi.

65. Ibid., cxlv.

66. Ibid., cliii.

67. Ibid., clxiv.

68. Spoleto, *Statutes* (1296) I:lxxi.

69. Ferrara, *Statutes* (1287) V:xvi, lv, cxxvii, cxliii, clxviii.

70. "This ditch and sewer should be constructed along the ditches situated at the side of the aforesaid road so that the aforesaid road and the homes situated along it are not flooded as they will continue to be if the sewer is not constructed." Ferrara, *Statutes* (1287) V:lxix, cxxv.

71. Bologna, *Statutes* (1288) X:vi, x.

72. Ferrara, *Statutes* (1287) V:lxxxvi.

Chapter Four

1. For our purposes, wells will be defined as "shafts for obtaining water vertically below the spot where it is required when it is not obvious at the surface." This will serve to distinguish wells from "holy wells," which were frequently nothing more than natural springs that were initially enclosed and later deepened. See R. J. Forbes, "Hydraulic Engineering and Sanitation," in Singer et al., *A History of Technology*, vol. 2, p. 633.

2. For example, the Aqua Appia was built c. 300 B.C.E. at public expense, the Anio Vetus c. 275 B.C.E. with the spoils taken from King Pyrrhus, and the Aqua Marcia in 146 B.C.E. with the booty taken from Carthage and Corinth.

3. See Vitruvius Pollio, *De Architectura* (On architecture), ed. and trans. Frank Granger (Cambridge, Mass., 1931–1934), bk. 8 (Loeb ed., 1934, vol. 2, pp. 132ff.); Frontinus, *De Aquae Ductu*, I, 16 (Loeb ed., vol. 2, pp. 356ff.).

4. The set of 25 gauges of standard pipes was based on the *quinaria*, that is, a pipe formed from a strip of lead five digits (9.2 cm, or 3.75 inches) wide; pipe sizes ranged in capacity from one *quinaria* to 120 *quinaria*.

5. Sextus Julius Frontinus, *The Stratagems*, and *The Aqueducts of Rome*, Eng. trans. Charles E. Bennett, trans. of *Aqueducts* a revision of Clemens Herschel translation, ed. Mary B. McElwain (Cambridge, Mass., 1950), II, 75, 112–116 (Loeb ed., 1925, pp. 404, 442ff.).

6. Vitruvius, *De Architectura*, VIII, iv, 1–2, as quoted in Smith, Wayte, and Marindin, *Antiquities*, vol. 2, p. 674.

7. Vitruvius, *De Architectura*, VIII, iv, 15, as quoted in Smith, Wayte, and Marindin, *Antiquities*, vol. 2.

8. The original dimensions of the Cloaca Maxima were twelve feet four inches in height and ten feet eight inches in width. The sewer is presently more than one-third filled with silt and mud, although it is still functional.

9. *Digesta Iustiniani*, 7.1.27, and 3; 30.1.39 and 5.

10. This project was begun in 41 C.E. under Emperor Claudius I and was completed some eleven years later by a workforce that was said to have exceeded 30,000 men. This project yielded 50,000 acres for the imperial domain. See Tacitus, *Annales*, XII, lvi (Loeb ed., 1937, vol. 2, p. 396ff.), and Suetonius, *Vitae* 12, *Caesarum*, v. See *Claudius*, xx, 1–2; xxi, 6 (Loeb ed., 1934, vol. 2, pp. 36ff., 43ff.).

11. Strabo, *Geography*, v, C213 (Loeb ed., 1923, vol. 2, pp. 312ff.).

12. Ibid., C217, p. 328. Roman engineers were less successful in their attempts to drain the Pontine marshes; some historians have seen a parallel between the strength of the City of Rome's municipal government, the incidence of malaria in Rome, and the efficiency of the system for draining the marshes. Weak, ineffective, tax-poor governments were unable to generate enough revenue to meet the costs incurred in the drainage program.

13. This "fossa marina" was navigable until the first century; see Plutarch, *Vitae parallelae: Caius Marius*, XV, 1–4 (Loeb ed., vol. 9, pp. 500ff.).

14. Tacitus, *Annales,* XI, xx (Loeb ed., vol. 3, p. 280).

15. Note, for example, Spoleto, *Statutes* (1296) XI and XII, in which specific persons are placed in charge of particular fountains.

16. Ferrara, *Statutes* (1287) IV:lxxv.

17. Ibid., lxxiii.

18. Ibid., lxxvi.

19. Ibid., lxxvii; V:xxxiii.

20. Ibid., V:xv, xxiii, xxvii, liv, lx, lxiii.

21. Ibid., xxxii.

22. Verona, *Statutes* (1276) IV:clxxiii.

23. Ibid., clxxvi.

24. Ibid., clxxviii, clxxix; Bassano also would not allow its craftsmen to throw wool or leather waste into the Brenta; Bassano, *Statutes* (1259) III:xxiii; (1295) II:xliii.

25. Verona, *Statutes* (1276) IV:clxxviii.

26. Ibid., clxxviii.

27. Ibid., clxxix; a desirable and probably intended result was the creation of a navigable waterway through which the residents would be able to ship their agricultural produce to the city.

28. Ibid.

29. Spoleto, *Statutes* (1296) I:xi.

30. Ibid., xii.

31. Ibid., xxi.

32. Spoleto, *Constitutum* (1296) I:xiii. See also Bassano, *Statutes* (1295) IV:xvii.

33. Bassano, *Statutes* (1295) I:xiiii.

34. Ibid.

35. Spoleto, *Breve* (1296), I:lxviii.

36. Spoleto, *Constitutum* (1296), I:liv.

37. Ibid., I:xii, xiv; II:xviii, li.

38. Ferrara, *Statutes* (1287) V:xviii, lix, cxi, clix, clxxvi, clxxvii; Bassano, *Statutes* (1259) V:l, lxv.

39. Ferrara, *Statutes* (1287) V:xviii, lviii, cxi, clix, clxxvi, clxxvii; Bassano, *Statutes* (1259) II:lxxii.

40. Verona, *Statutes* (1276) IV:clxxii, clxxxvii, clxxxix, ccxvii; Bologna, *Statutes* (1288) X:vi, vii, viii, x, lxxvi; Ferrara, *Statutes* (1287) II:ccxcix, ccci, cd; V:vi, cxlii; Bassano, *Statutes* (1259) II:lxx, lxxi.

41. Verona, *Statutes* (1276) IV:clxxxix, clxxxix, cc; Ferrara, *Statutes* (1287) V:l, lxv.

42. Ferrara, *Statutes* (1287) V:xcvi, cxii, cxxvii.

43. Verona, *Statutes* (1276) IV:cc, ccvii; Ferrara, *Statutes* (1287) V:xvi, clxi.

44. Verona, *Statutes* (1276) IV:clxxxvii, ccvi; Ferrara, *Statutes* (1287) V:xx, xlviii, cxviii, cxlii, clix.

45. Verona, *Statutes* (1276) IV:cci; Ferrara, *Statutes* (1287) V:lx, lxiii.

46. Verona, *Statutes* (1276) IV:clxx; Ferrara, *Statutes* (1287) V:xvii, liv; Bassano, *Statutes* (1259) II:lxxi; (1295) II:xli.

47. The statute makers make frequent reference to the concern that neighbors and passersby should not have to pass by outfalls or through the contents of sewers and drains. Piran, *Statutes* (1307) I:viii, xxiii; Spoleto, *Breve* (1296) I:lxi; Bologna, *Statutes* (1288) X:ii, xxii; IV:cix, cx, cxi; Bassano, *Statutes* (1259) II:xxxix, lxxiii; IV:lviii; *Statutes* (1295) II:xliii, xliv, xlv, xlix; III:xii; IV:xiv; Ferrara, *Statutes* (1287) V:xxvii, xxviii, xxix, xxx, xliii, lxiii, xcvi.

48. Ferrara, *Statutes* (1287) V:v, lxxv, lxxvi, c, cvii, clxxix.

49. Spoleto, *Constitutum* (1296) I:lvii.

50. Spoleto, *Breve* (1296) I:lii, lvii, lxix; *Constitutum* (1296) I:xl; II:iv, xiv, xxxix.

51. Spoleto, *Statutes* (1296) I:lxxi.

52. Spoleto, *Constitutum* (1296) I:lxxxiii. Since most communes charged tolls to use the bridges, one might speculate about whether the communes were as concerned with the potential loss of revenue as people bypassed the bridge to cross the now dry riverbed as they were with the problem of flooding. See also Bologna, *Statutes* (1288) X:xxxviii.

53. See, for example, Ferrara, *Statutes* (1287) V:i-xi; V:xii.

54. Ferrara, *Statutes* (1287) V:vii, xi.

55. "The Procurators of the Commune of Verona are required and should see to it that the water of the fountain of the Poianum flow through its customary places. Likewise we ordain that the Procurators of the Commune of Verona, within two months of [the beginning of] their terms of office, are required to and should take care and see to it that the water of the fountain of Poianum should flow through a suitable and customary streambed to its outflow so that it should not cause a loss by going out of its streambed; each and every one of the aforesaid procurators is required by those who have sustained a loss because that water has gone beyond its streambed, and obliged to take care and see to it that this [flooding] does not take place; and, those who are discovered taking water from the streambed or who are found damaging the streambed so that the water does not run down through it, should pay a fine of 100 Veronese soldi to the Commune of Verona for each and every offense, and they should reimburse [the loss] to those who have suffered it. And, anyone may be an accuser; half of the fine belongs to the Commune and the other half to the accuser. And, [it is understood] that the commune and men of Poianum are required to and should take diligent care lest the aforesaid water be taken from the aforesaid streambed, and they are required to pay the aforesaid fine, if they do not present those persons who have taken the water from the stream, as often as the aforesaid water is taken from the aforesaid stream, and they should have legal recourse against those persons who had taken water from the streambed." Verona, *Statutes* (1276) IV:clxxiv, clxxvii.

56. Ferrara, *Statutes* (1287) V:i.

57. Ibid., iv.

58. Ibid., x, lxxxi.

59. Ibid., lxxxiii.

60. Ibid., vii, xx, l, lvi, lxii, lxiv, lxvii, lxxxiii.

61. Ibid., ix, lxxix, lxxxv, xcii, xcv, cii, cv, cvi.

62. "And, First, Concerning the Sworn Oath of the Judge of the Embankments.

I, the Judge of the Embankments, in good faith and without deceit, to defend and protect that noble man, the Lord Marquis, and his sons, in all of his honors, jurisdictions, privileges, and holdings and to maintain all of the embankments and banks of the Po River in the City of Ferrara and its District; . . . I will not undertake a project at the wish or insistence of any person or persons, unless it is in accord with that which I believe is expedient for the good [of the Commune of Ferrara], so that in all of the works pertaining to my office, I will consider only the public good. . . . I will not tarry outside of the City of Ferrara, unless it is according to that which I consider necessary and useful for the public good. I will accept nothing by myself or through any intermediary, official or otherwise, as a gift, exchange, or accomodation, and I will not be detered from my duty by the name of any other person or by any person of the City of Ferrara or its District. In no way will I accept food or drink in a small or large quantity. If I should have known or could have known that any one of my officials has received something more for his duty than the salary established for us, I will denounce such a person to the Podesta of the City of Ferrara as soon as I can" (Ferrara, *Statutes* (1287) V:i, iv, v, viii, xi, xii).

Chapter Five

1. P. J. Jones, *Cambridge Economic History of Europe*, 2d ed., vol. 1 (Cambridge, 1952–1966), p. 348.

2. R. A. de Roover, in *The Rise and Decline of the Medici Bank, 1397–1494* (Cambridge, 1963), has written that in 1457 the Florentine families could be divided into four groups: the rich, 2 percent; the middle class, 16 percent; the poor, 54 percent; and the destitute, 28 percent, as mentioned in Hohenberg and Lees, *The Making of Urban Europe, 1000–1950*, p. 45. Note also: "For although the city council restored the Council of the People to its pre-plague size of fifty per terzo in 1353 (having reduced it by one third), its composition remained unchanged. Tradition was served, but any desires within the lower ranks of the *popolo* for greater participation in government were stymied" (Bowsky, *A Medieval Italian Commune*, p. 41). Daniel Waley, in *The Italian City-Republics* (Reprint, New York, 1978), p. 183, argued that the *popolo* leadership was provided by educated professional elites and prominent and well-to-do guildsmen, but the really humble were only to be employed in armed conflict; Martines, *Power and Imagination*, p. 63, would agree. If one wishes to look at specific numbers, Herlihy, *Pisa*, pp. 128–129 found 1,188 artisans in the city in 1288, broken down into the following categories: professional (notaries, lawyers, doctors), 147; food (grain, wine, meat), 346; building and metallurgy, 289; leather and skins, 305; and textiles (linen,

wool, dying, tailoring), 101. The 1,188 were out of a total population of 12,500 citizens and a population of 38,000 in 1293 (p. 36).

3. Waley, *Italian City-Republics*, p. 183.

4. See John Kenneth Hyde, *Padua in the Age of Dante* (New York, 1966), p. 243.

5. Giovani Villani, *Cronica*, bk. 2, chap. 94, as quoted in Carlo M. Cipolla, *Before the Industrial Revolution: European Society and Economy, 1000–1700* (New York, 1976), p. 195.

6. Jean Gimpel, *The Medieval Machine: The Industrial Revolution of the Middle Ages* (New York, 1976), p. 85.

7. Michael M. Postan, *The Medieval Economy and Society: An Economic History of Britain in the Middle Ages* (Reprint, New York, 1984), pp. 255ff.

8. William M. Bowsky, *The Finance of the Commune of Siena, 1287–1355* (Oxford, 1970), p. 143.

9. Ibid., p. 144.

10. The bakers also saw this possibility and maintained control over the gabelle from 1297 to 1314 (Ibid., p. 140).

11. Ibid., p. 142; and there is some evidence that this practice occurred after 1318 when the guild was suppressed by commune authorities for its participation in rebellion.

12. It is also interesting to note that two of the more prominent tax farmers, notably, Cione del fu Vitaluccio and his brothers, and Giovanni Salimbeni, played vital roles in the Great Rebellion of 1318. Bowsky also felt that the legal restrictions on the butchers were a prime cause of their rebellion. See William M. Bowsky, "The Anatomy of Rebellion in Fourteenth-Century Siena: From Commune to Signory," in Lauro Martines, *Violence and Civil Disorder in Italian Cities, 1200–1500* (Berkeley, 1972), pp. 245–246.

13. David Herlihy, "Population, Plague, and Social Change in Rural Pistoia, 1201–1430," *Economic History Review*, 2d ser., 18 (1965), pp. 230ff.

14. Ferrara, *Statutes* (1287) II:xxvii.

15. Ibid.; note also: "No foodstuffs, living or dead, should be carried outside of the District of Ferrara by any native-born person or by any foreigner; anyone who goes against this statute is fined in the amount of five *soldi* of Ferrarese money for each pound of the value of the aforesaid foodstuffs and the foodstuffs themselves are to be reported and fall into the possession of the Commune. If, however, the aforesaid foodstuffs should not have been found, the lawbreaker is fined to the amount of the value of those goods at the rate of five *soldi* of Ferrarese money for each pound" (Ferrara, *Statutes* (1287) II:xxv).

16. See, for example, Bassano, *Statutes* (1295) III:xxiii; Verona, *Statutes* (1276) IV: ix.

17. Verona, *Statutes* (1276) IV:clvii and clviii.

18. Ferrara, *Statutes* (1287) IV:x; see also IV:xv.

19. Bassano, *Statutes* (1295) III:xxi.

20. Ibid.

21. Ibid., xxiii.

22. Bassano, *Statutes* (1259) I:ix.

23. Ibid.

24. Ibid., II:xxx.

25. Bassano, *Statutes* (1295) I:xx.

26. Verona, *Statutes* (1276) IV:lxiii; the Ferrarese enacted a similar set of regulations, see Ferrara, *Statutes* (1287) II:ccxcvii ff.

27. Verona, *Statutes* (1276) IV:lxv.

28. Ibid., lxvii, lxix, lxx.

29. Ibid., lxv, lxxi.

30. Ibid., lxxi–lxxvi.

31. Ibid., lxxviii.

32. Ibid., lxxxi.

33. Ibid., lxxix, lxxx.

34. Piran, *Statutes* (1307) III:vi; VI:iv.

35. Ferrara, *Statutes* (1287) II:ccxlvii.

36. Verona, *Statutes* (1276) IV:lxxix.

37. Ibid., lxxx.

38. Verona, *Statutes* (1276) II:cccii; the same statute also informed Veronese citizens that no one could be forced to enter the butchers' guild, unless it was his wish, provided that those (nonguild) butchers made good and legal meats and sold them legally. Bologna, *Statutes* (1288) X:iii.

39. See Chapter 2 for extensive information on the regulations restricting butchers, fishermen, merchants, leather workers, and clothiers.

40. Ferrara, *Statutes* (1287) IV:lxxvii.

41. Verona, *Statutes* (1276) IV:clxxix.

42. Bassano, *Statutes* (1259) IV: cxxxvii.

43. Ferrara, *Statutes* (1287) II:ccciv.

44. Ibid., cccv.

45. Ibid., cccvi.

46. Ibid.

47. Ibid., cccvii, cccviii, cccx.

48. Ibid., cccix.

49. Ibid., cccx.

50. Verona, *Statutes* (1276) IV:lxxxvii, lxxxviii, xc, xcii.

51. Ibid., lxxxvii.

52. Ibid., lxxxix.

53. Ibid., lxxxviii.

54. Ibid., xci.

55. Verona, *Statutes* (1276) IV:lxxxviii.

56. Ferrara, *Statutes* (1287) IV:lxxvi.

57. Piran, *Statutes* (1307) X:vii, viii, ix, x.

58. The Piranese quartermaster was responsible for collecting all of the commune's grain, storing it, and distributing it to appointed bakers for milling, bak-

ing, and sale as bread. Piran, *Statutes* (1307) I:vi, viii, xxvii; see also Bassano, *Statutes* (1259) I:viii.

59. See, for example, Bassano, *Statutes* (1259) I:vii; (1295) III:xxviii.

60. See, for example, Bassano, *Statutes* (1259) I:vii–viii; Verona, *Statutes* (1276) IV:ix.

61. Herlihy, "Rural Pistoia," pp. 236ff.

62. Herlihy argued in ibid. that rural Italian populations were in decline at least half a century before the onset of the Black Death because of economic conditions that made familial fertility and early marriage unlikely prospects for rural people.

63. Spoleto, *Breve* (1296) I:lxix.

64. Piran, *Statutes* (1307) I:xii.

65. Ibid., IX:xxxv.

66. Ferrara, *Statutes* (1287) II:xxiii, xxv, xxvii; Verona, *Statutes* (1276) IV:ix.

67. Verona, *Statutes* (1276) IV:cxlvii.

68. Ibid., clv, clvi.

69. Ibid., clvii.

70. Ibid., clviii.

71. Ibid.

72. A partial list of the cleaning agents used in medieval crafts would include the following: soda and potash (from sodium carbonate, plant ashes, and calcined tartar), tartar or argol (a potassium hydrogen tartrate deposited in wine casks), ammonia (from stale urine), lime (chalk or limestone burned in kilns), cleansing agents (such as oil, bran, sand, ashes, pumices, and certain plant juices), fuller's earth, nitric acid, aqua regia (a hydrochloric–nitric acid mixture), and sulfuric acid.

73. Bassano, *Statutes* (1295) II:xliii; Verona, *Statutes* (1276) IV:clxxviii, clxxix.

74. Bassano, *Statutes* (1295) II:xlix.

75. Ferrara, *Statutes* (1287) IV:lxxv.

Chapter Six

1. Martines, *Power and Imagination,* pp. 60, 162ff.; Robert S. Gottfried, *The Black Death: Natural and Human Disaster in Medieval Europe* (New York, 1983), pp. 18ff.; Herlihy, *Pistoia,* pp. 133–137, and *Pisa,* pp. 109, 125–129, 159; Hyde, *Society and Politics,* pp. 26–28.

2. Herlihy, *Pistoia,* chapter 3 and especially p. 77, and *Pisa,* pp. x–xi, 36; Martines, *Power and Imagination,* p. 163; Hyde, *Society and Politics,* pp. 74ff.

3. David Herlihy and Christine Klapisch-Zuber, in *Tuscans and Their Families: A Study of the Florentine Catasto of 1427* (New Haven, 1985), pp. 14, 117–120, indicate the presence of substantial numbers of sharecroppers by the early 1400s, basing that conclusion on the outflow of urban capital into the *contado* to purchase land, implements, buildings, etc. This process accelerated after the advent of the Black Death because of the scarcity of labor and the general decline of population.

See also Enrico Fiumi, *Demographia, movimento urbanistico e classi sociali in Prato dall'eta' communale al tempi moderni* (Florence, 1968), p. 140.

4. Herlihy, *Pistoia*, p. 124, and *Pisa*, pp. 117ff.

5. Gottfried, *Black Death*, pp. 28ff. Famines struck in 1291–1293, 1304, 1305, 1309–1319, 1324–1325, 1330–1334, 1344, 1349–1351, 1358–1360, 1371, 1373–1374, and 1390.

6. Bergamo (Italy), *Statuta magnificae civitatis Bergomi* (Bergamo, 1727; reprint, Arnoldo Forni, 1981), hereafter cited as *Statutes of 1727*.

7. *Statutes of 1727*, VII:i.

8. Ibid.

9. Statute 2, mentioned further on, permitted individual farmers to sell grains and legumes out of their homes; thus, it was expected that they would have a personal interest in maintaining a higher standard of cleanliness.

10. Collation 8 contains most of the street and sanitary legislation. A common feature is the requirement that local citizens and governing bodies keep streets and roads free and clean of debris at their own expense. A collation is a collection of laws loosely grouped by a common theme.

11. *Statutes of 1727*, VII:cxxiv.

12. Ibid., cxxi.

13. Ibid., cxxvii.

14. Statute 127 specifically directs millers not to adulterate ground flour or corn meal with such materials as sand, chaff, or weeds; and Statutes 129 and 130 made millers responsible for transporting grain and flour to and from mills covered in such a way as to prevent contamination.

15. Roman authorities faced a similar problem. The conversion of cropland to pastureland produced shortfalls in critical food crops and required the authorities to import food. Medieval Italian authorities were also required to import food, in some cases, from as far away as North Africa. Hence, the municipal statutes reflect a heavy dependence upon food regulations designed to conserve both the food and the local agricultural resource base.

16. The sheer magnitude of the problem facing medieval municipal officials is almost beyond the comprehension of their modern counterparts and it continued for a long time afterward. Black-and-white photographs of nineteenth- and early twentieth-century streets, obviously taken during the summer months, frequently depict large piles of animal waste and debris, reminiscent of the snow piles left curbside after the passage of snowplows in the winter. This problem persisted until the advent of the widespread use of mechanical power.

17. *Statutes of 1727*, VII:cxlvii.

18. Ibid., VII:cxlix.

19. Bowsky, *Medieval Italian Commune*, pp. 131ff., has described an attempted coup d'état in 1318 by dissidents, led by the butchers and an aristocratic faction, and reported the following "battle cry," "*Viva il popolo* and the guilds, and death to those who starve us!" Severe restrictions were placed subsequently on the butchers' rights to organize and practice their trade.

20. Statute 168 prohibits salted fish from being sold at a price higher than permitted by the *calmedrium*, or concession, auctioned off by the commune at the beginning of Lent each year.

21. An imperial pound was a reckoning or accounting measure rather than actual coinage. In terms of relative value, an average tradesman earned 3 to 4 pounds per year.

22. *Statutes of 1727*, VII:clxxxii.

23. *Putredo*, associated with the term *putor*, is defined as "rottenness, putridity, and foul smelling." *Abominatio* is derived from the verb *abominor*, which means to abominate, abhor, or detest.

24. These trades included apothecaries, kettle makers, shoemakers, skinners, papermakers, and others working with the kinds of chemicals associated with the leather-making craft.

25. Bologna, *Statutes of 1288*, X:ii, xxii, IV:cix, cx, cxi.

26. Ibid., X:iii; Bassano had a similar problem in 1259 and had to address it again in its statute revision of 1295 (Bassano, *Statutes of 1295*, I:xx).

27. Collation 8 contains most of Bergamo's legislation regarding streets, roads, bridges, waterways, and related urban infrastructure.

28. *Statutes of 1727*, VIII:iii.

29. Ibid., i; this statute also provided a working definition for a major road of the commune, i.e., "major roads are all roads having an entrance and an exit in a public place, or onto the public roads, or having an entrance at the churches."

30. A fuller's perch is the bar or frame that supports the cloth while the nap is being raised.

31. A definition of the chief workman or his duties does not appear in the statutes, but it is clear that he was probably a civil engineer employed by the commune to oversee construction projects.

32. *Statutes of 1727*, VIII:vi.

33. Ibid., xx; Statute 21 provides a similar procedure and right of condemnation for those seeking easements for roadways.

34. The podesta could lose up to four months of his annual salary if he did not enforce the law (see Statute 76) and the lords judges of the streets could lose 25 imperial pounds if they did not perform their duties.

35. *Statutes of 1727*, VIII:lxxiii.

36. Ibid., lxxvii.

37. Ibid., lxxxiv.

38. Ibid., lxxxii.

39. Ibid., lxxxviii, lxxxix.

40. Ibid., lxxxv.

41. Rector is another title for the Venetian podesta.

42. *Statutes of 1727*, VIII:xi.

43. Ibid., xi.

44. Ibid., xiv.

45. Ibid., xvii.

Select Bibliography

Published Manuscript Sources

Agleardi, C. *Raccolta d'documenti riguardanti la Storia di Bergamo dal 1402 sino al 1502 inclusive.* Exerpta xx Pergami. Estratti riguardenti la storia antica di Bergami, ms. in Bergamo Biblioteca Civica. Gab, Gamma 5.6/1 (= MMB 403), f. 152r–157r (1509, 3 and 24 July).

Agnoletti, Anna Maria E. *Statuto dell'Arte della Lana di Firenze, 1317–1319.* Florence, 1940–1958.

Alessandrini, Armando. *Statuti di Monteprandone, 1537.* Teramo, 1976.

Antiga, Luigi. *Gli statuti di Filetto del 1296.* Villa Franca, 1973.

Antonelli, Giovanni. *Statuti di Spoleto del 1296.* Florence, 1962.

Azioni del Comune di Bergamo. Bergamo, Biblioteca Civica, Sala I, D.8.6.

Banchi, Luciano. *Breve degli Officiali del Comune di Siena compilato nell'anno MCCL al Tempo del Podesta Ubertino da Lando di Piacenza.* Vol. 3. Siena, 1865.

Barelli, Giuseppe. *Statuti di Pamparato.* Turin, 1965.

Becattini, Vincenzo. *Libro degli statuti del Comune di Modigliana, 1384–1762.* Faenza, 1986.

Bergamo (Italy). *Statuta magnificae civitatis Bergomi.* Bergamo, 1727; reprint, Arnoldo Forni, 1981.

_____. *Statuti Bergomi.* Brescia: per Angelum and Iacobum fratres de Britannicis, 1491.

Berlan, Francesco. *Le due edizioni milanese e torinese della Consuetudini di Milano del'anno 1215, cenni ed appunti.* Venice, 1872.

_____. *Liber consuetudinum Mediolani anni 1216.* Milan, 1866.

_____. *Statuti di Pistoia del secolo XII reintegrati.* Bologna, 1882.

Besta, Enrico, and Gian Luigi Barni. *Liber Consuetudinum Mediolani Anni MCCXVI.* Rome, 1949.

Betto, Bianca. *Gli statuti del comune di Treviso (sec. XIII–XIV).* Rome: Fonti per la storia d'Italia pubblicate dall'Istituto storico italiano per il Medio Evo 109, pt. 1, 1984.

Bizzarri, Dina. *Gli statuti del comune di Torino del 1360.* Turin: Deputazione subalpina di storia patria Biblioteca, 138, 1933.

Bonaini, Francesco. *Statuti inediti della citta di Pisa del XII al XIV secolo.* Florence, 1870.

Bortolami, Sante. *Territorio e societa in un comune rurale veneto (sec. XI–XIII): Pernumia e I suoi statuti.* Venice: Miscellanea di studi e memorie 18, 1978.

Caggese, R. *Statuti della Repubblica fiorentina. I: Capitano del popolo, 1322–1325; II: Podesta, 1325.* Florence, 1910–1921.

Cecchi, Dante. *Gli statuti di Apiro dell'anno 1388.* Padua: Pubblicazioni della Facolta di giurisprudenza, Universita di Macerata, Fonti 1, 1984.

———. *Gli statuti: di Sefro (1423), Fiastre (1436), Serra-petrona (1473), Campo rotondo (1475).* Macerata: Deputazione di storia per le Marche Studi e testi, 7, 1971.

Charybus, Alphonsus. *Consuetudines Nobilis Civitatis Messabae suique nunc postremo diligentissime repurgatae.* Venice, 1575.

Ciampi, Ignazio. *Cronache e statuti della citta di Viterbo.* Florence: Documenti di storia italiana, vol. 5, 1872.

Colombo, Franco. *Gli statuti di Muggia del 1420.* Trieste: Fonti e studi per la storia della Venezia Giulia, Serie prima, Fonti vol. 2, 1971.

Corsi, Domenico. *Statuti Urbanistici Medievali di Lucca gli Statu e de'Pubblici di Lucca nei secoli XII–XIV Curia del Fondaco.* Venice, 1960.

Doria, Gianni Penzo, and Sergio Perini. *Statuti e capitolari di Chioggia del 1272–1279; con le aggiunte fino al 1327.* Venice, 1993.

Fabbri, Carlo. *Statuti e riforme del Comune di terranuova 1487–1675: Una communita del contado fiorentino attraverso le sue instituzioni.* Florence: Biblioteca storica toscana, 25, 1989.

Fasoli, Gina. *Statuti del Comune di Bassano dell'anno 1259 dell'anno 1295.* Venice, 1940.

Fasoli, Gina, and Pietro Sella. *Statuti di Bologna dell'anno 1288.* 2 vols. Vatican City, 1937.

Fiemi, Luigi. *Codice Diplomatico della Citta d'Orvieto: Documenti e Registi dal Secolo XI al XV, e la Carta de Populo: Codice Statutario de Comune di Orvieto.* Florence, 1884.

De Franceschi, Camillo. *Gli Statuti del Comune di Pirano del 1307 confrontati quelli del 1332 e del 1358.* Vol. 14. Venice, 1960.

Frati, Luigi. *Monumenti pertinenti alla storia della provincia Romagna.* Rome, 1836–1864.

———. *Statuti di Bologna dall'anno 1245 all'anno 1267.* 3 vols. Bologna, 1869–1877.

Friuli (Italy). *Statuti della patria del Friuli.* Udine, 1717.

Gabrielli, Attilio. *Gli statuti di Velletri.* Velletri, 1912.

Gar, Tommasco, and Simone Cresseri. *Statuti della Citta di Riva, 1274–1790.* Trento, 1861.

Gaudenzi, Augusto. *Statuti del populo di Bologna del secolo XIII; gli ordinamenti sacrati e sacratissimi colle riformagioni da loro occasionate e dipendenti ed altri provvedimenti affini pubblicati per cura di Augusto Gaudenzi.* Bologna: Dei monumenti Serie I, 1888.

_____. *Statuti delle societa del popolo di Bologna.* Rome: Istituto storico italiano per il Medio Evo Fonti per la storia d'Italia, vols. 3–4. Forzani, Tip. del Senato, 1889–1896.

Gioacchini, Delfo. *Statuti dell citta di Orte.* Orte, 1981.

Gloria, Andrea. *Statuti del Comune di Padova dal Secolo XII all'anno 1285.* Padua, 1873.

Gualazzini, Ugo. *Gli statuti di Cremona del MCCCXXXIX e di Viadana del secolo XIV; contributi alla teoria generale degli statuti.* Milan: Corpus statuorum, 2–3, 1953–1954.

Imberciadori, Ildebrando. *Statuti del Comune Montepescali, 1427.* Siena, 1938.

_____. *Statuti di castel del Piano sul Monte Amiata (1571).* Florence: Fonti sui comuni rurali toscana, 8, 1980.

Laderchi, Cammillo. *Statuti di Ferrara dell'anno 1288.* Bologna, 1864–.

Lampertico, Fedele. *Statuti del Comune di Vicenza.* Venice, 1886.

Lusini, Alexander. *Il costituto del comune di Siena rigolarizzato nel MCCCIX–MCCCX.* 2 vols. Siena, 1903.

Lusardi, Aldo, and Erico Besta. *Statuta Veglae.* Corpus Statutorum Italicorum vol. 22, Terza Serie, Citta di Castello, 1945.

Macerata (Italy). *Volumen statutorum civitatis Maceratae (Macerata, 1553).* Sala Bolognese, 1983.

Manente, Stephania. *Statuti di Aviano del 1403.* Rome, 1990.

Mazzi, A. *Lo statuto del 1263.* Bergamo, 1902.

Montorsi, William. *Statuta Ferrariae Anno MCCLXXXVII.* Ferrara, 1955.

Morandini, Francesca. *Statuti delle Arti delgi Oliandoli e Pizzicagnoli e dei Beccai di Firenze: 1318–1346.* Florence, 1961.

Padua (Italy). *Statuti del Comune dal secolo XII all'anno 1285.* Padua, 1873.

Papaleoni, Giuseppe. *Gli statuti di Tione dal sec. XVI al XVIII.* Venice, 1895.

Parcianello, Frederica. *Statuti di Rovereto del 1425: Con le aggiunte dal 1434 al 1538.* Venice, 1991.

Pene-Vidari, Gian Savino. *Statuti del Comune di Ivrea.* Turin: Deputazione sub alpina di storia patria. Biblioteca storica subalpina, 185–186, 188, 1968–1974.

Peter, Marquis of Fulx. *Statutorum Magnificae Civitatis Belluni Libri Quinque.* Venice, 1747.

Pinerolo, Francesco Cognasso. *Statuti civili del comune di Chieri (1313).* Pavia: Biblioteca della Societa storica subalpina, 76, Deputazione subalpina di storia patria. Biblioteca storica subalpina, 182, 1958.

Podestaria e capitanato (Bergamo, Italy). *Podestaria e capitanato di Bergamo.* Relazioni dei rettori in terraferma, 12. Milan, 1978.

Poma, Cesare. *Gli statuti del comune di Biella del 1245.* Biella, 1885.

Riccius, Bernardinus. *Statuta magnificae civitatis Bergomi.* Bergamo, 1727.

Sacco, Rodolfo. *Statuti di Revello, 1396–1477.* Bene Vagienna, 1945.

Sandri, Gino. *Gli Statuti Veronesi del 1276 colle correzioni e le aggiunte fino al 1323.* Vol. 3. Venice, 1940.

Sartini, Ferdinando. *Statuti dell'Arte dei Rigattieri e Linaioli di Firenze, 1296–1340.* Florence, 1940–1958.

Sella, Pietro. *Statuta Comunis Bugelle e Documenta Adiecta.* Biella, 1904.

Selvatico, P. *Statuti del Comune di Padova dal secolo XII all'anno 1285.* Padua, 1876.

Simbenius, Johannes. *Leges Statutae Reipublicae Sancti Marini.* Forolivii, 1884.

Sinatti D'Amico, Franca. *Statuto di San Vito all'incisa (1379).* Florence, 1970.

Solazzi, Gino. *Liber Statutorum Comunis Vitellianae.* Milan, 1951.

Statuti di Belluno. Venice, 1747.

Statuti 1333 (Bergamo, April, 1333), ms. in Bergamo, Biblioteca Civica, Sala I, D.9.19.

Statuti 1353 (Bergamo), ms. in Bergamo, Biblioteca Civica, Sala I, D.6.1.

Statuti 1371 (Bergamo), ms. in Bergamo, Biblioteca Civica, Sala I, D.7.29.

Statuti 1391 (Bergamo), ms. in Bergamo, Biblioteca Civica, Sala I, D.9.6, and another ms. in Bergamo Biblioteca Radini Tedeschi, S. Alessandro in Clero, 117.

Statuti 1422 (Bergamo), ms. in Bergamo, Biblioteca Civica, Sala I, D.7.27.

Statuti 1430 (Bergamo), ms. in Bergamo, Biblioteca Civica, Sala I, D.7.35.

Statuti 1491, Statuta communitatis Bergomi. Brescia, 1491.

Stefani, Pietro De. *Miane della Valmareno nel trecento: Il testamento di Pre Jacobino da Miane, Statuti e officiali della Valmareni, La Pieve e il comune rurali di Miane, Miane el il Monstero di Follina, Poli di vita mianese . . .* Venice, 1980.

Storti Storchi, Claudia. *Lo statuto di Bergamo del 1331.* Fontes Pavia-Milano, Fonti storico-giuridiche, Statuti, 1. Milan, 1986.

Szombathely, Marino de. *Statuti di Trieste de 1350.* Trieste, 1930.

––––––. *Statuti di Trieste de 1421.* Trieste, 1935.

Tarlazzi, Antonio. *Statuti del comune di Ravenna.* Ravenna: Monumenti istorici pertinenti alle provincie di Romegna, ser. 1. Calderini, 1886.

Udine (Italy). *Statuta et ordinamenti comunitatis terre Utini MCCCCXXV: statuti e ordinamenti del comune di Udine.* Udine: pubblicati dal municipio per cura della Commissione preposta al Civico museo e biblioteca, 1898.

Vaglia, Ugo. *Statuti rurali di Anfo, Darfo e Darzo dei secoli XV–XVI.* Brescia, 1969.

Vailetti, Johannis Baptista Peter, and Hiermus de Alexandro. *Statuta Magnificae Civitatis Bergomi.* Bergamo, 1727.

Zanetti, Ginevra, ed. *Statuti di Bagolino; statuta primaeva et antiquissima comunitatis Bagolini, primitus correcta anno domini M.CD.LXX.III.* Brescia, 1935.

Zdekauer, Lodovico. *Breve et Ordinamenta Populi Pistorii anni MCCLXXXIV.* Milan, 1891.

––––––. *Statuti del Commune di Siena fino alla redazione del 1262.* Milan, 1897.

––––––. *Statutum potestatis communis Pistorii anni MCCLXXXVI.* Milan, 1888.

––––––. *Sugli Statuti piu antichi del Comune di Montolmo.* Rome, 1909.

Zdekauer, Lodovico, and Pietro Sella. *Statuti di Ascoli Piceno dell'anno MCC-CLXXVII.* Rome: Fonti per la storia d'Italia pubblicate dall'Istituto storico italiano. Statuti Secolo XIV, Forzani e c., tipografia del Senato, 1910.

Zoli, Andrea, ed. *Statuto del secolo XIII del commune di Ravenna.* Ravenna, 1904.

Zoli, Franca Zerboni. *Statuti di San Godenzo (1413–1613).* Commune di San Godenzo, 1985.

Urban, Legal, and Environmental History

Abrams, Philip, and E. A. Wrigley, eds. *Towns in Societies: Essays in Economic History and Historical Sociology.* Cambridge, 1979.

Bautier, Robert-Henri. *The Economic Development of Medieval Europe.* London, 1971.

Becker, Marvin B. *Medieval Italy: Constraints and Creativity.* Bloomington, Ind., 1981.

Berger, Adolf. *Encyclopedic Dictionary of Roman Law.* Philadelphia, 1953.

Bertelli, Sergio. *Il potere oligarchico nello stato-citta' medievale.* Florence, 1978.

Boutruche, R. *Signoria e feudalesimo.* Bologna, 1971.

Bowsky, William M. *A Medieval Italian Commune: Siena Under the Nine, 1287–1355.* Berkeley, 1981.

_____. "*The Buon Governo of Siena,* 1287–1355: A Medieval Italian Oligarchy." *Speculum* 37 (1962), 368–381.

_____. "City and Contado: Military Relationships and Communal Bonds in Fourteenth-Century Siena." In *Renaissance Studies in Honor of Hans Baron,* ed. Anthony Molho and John A. Tedeschi, Florence, 1971.

_____. "The Constitution and Administration of a Tuscan Republic in the Middle Ages and Early Renaissance: The *Maggior Sindaco* in Siena." *Studi Senesi* 80 (1968), 7–22.

_____. *The Finance of the Commune of Siena, 1287–1355.* Oxford, 1970.

_____. "The Impact of the Black Death upon Sienese Government and Society." *Speculum* 37 (1962), 368–381.

_____. "The Medieval Commune and Internal Violence: Police Power and Public Safety in Siena, 1287–1355." *American Historical Review* 73 (1967), 1–17.

_____. "Medieval Citizenship: The Individual and the State in the Commune of Siena, 1287–1355." *Studies in Medieval and Renaissance History* 4 (1967), pp. 193–243.

Brentari, Ottone. *Storia di Bassano e del suo Territorio.* Bassano, 1884; reprint, 1980.

Butler, W. F. *The Lombard Communes: A History of the Republics of North Italy.* Westport, Conn., 1969.

Calisse, Carlo. *A History of Italian Law.* The Continental Legal History Series, vol. 8. New York, 1969.

Carbone, S. *Provveditori e Sopraprovveditori alla Sanita della Repubblica di Venice.* Rome, 1962.

Carocci, Sandro. "Le comunalie di Orvieto fra la fine dell XII e la meta del XIV secolo." *Mélanges Ecole français Rome. Moyen Age. Temps modern* 99 (2) (1987), 701–728.

Cenci, Cesare. "Le Costitutzioni Padovane del 1310." *Archives français historique* 76 (October–December 1983), 505–588.

Cipolla, Carlo M. *Before the Industrial Revolution: European Society and Economy, 1000–1700.* New York, 1976.

_____. *Cristofano and the Plague: A Study in the History of Public Health in the Age of Galileo.* Berkeley, 1973.

_____. *Faith, Reason, and the Plague in Seventeenth-Century Tuscany.* Trans. Muriel Kittel. Ithaca, 1977.

_____. *Fighting the Plague in Seventeenth-Century Italy.* Madison, Wis., 1981.

_____. *Public Health and the Medical Profession in the Renaissance.* New York, 1976.

Cosgrove, John Joseph. *A History of Sanitation.* Pittsburgh, 1909.

Cracco Ruggini, Lellia, and Giorgio Cracco. "Changing Fortunes of the Italian City from Late Antiquity to Early Middle Ages." *Rivista Filologia Istruzione Classica* 105 (4) (1977), 425–489.

Cuomo, Luisa. "Sul commercio dei panni a Bologna nel 1270." *Archivio storico italiano* 135 (3–4) (1977), 333–372.

Dahl, Robert A. "A Critique of the Ruling Elite Model." *American Political Science Review* 52 (1958), 452—465.

Dowd, Douglas F. "Power and Economic Development: The Rise and Fall of Medieval Bologna." *Journal of European Economic History* 3 (fall 1974), 411–433.

Dunin-Wasowicz, Teresa. "Climate as a Factor Affecting the Human Environment in the Middle Ages." *Journal of European Economic History* 4 (winter 1975), 244–250.

Dyer, Christopher. "The Consumer and the Market in the Later Middle Ages." *Economic History Review* 42 (August 1989), 305–327.

Fiumi, Enrico. *Demographia, movimento urbanistico e classi sociali in Prato dall'eta' communale al tempi moderni.* Florence, 1968.

_____. *Storia economica e sociale di San Gimigrano.* Florence, 1961.

Fustel De Coulanges, Numa Denis. *The Ancient City: A Study on the Religion, Laws, and Institutions of Greece and Rome.* Baltimore, 1980.

Garnsey, Peter. *Famine and Food Supply in the Graeco-Roman World.* Cambridge, 1988.

Gimpel, Jean. *The Medieval Machine: The Industrial Revolution of the Middle Ages.* New York, 1976.

Glacken, Clarence J. *Traces on the Rhodian Shore: Nature and Culture in Western Thought from Ancient Times to the End of the Eighteenth Century.* Berkeley, 1976.

Goffart, Walter A. *Rome's Fall and After.* London, 1989.

Gottfried, Robert S. *The Black Death: Natural and Human Disaster in Medieval Europe.* New York, 1983.

Grubb, James S. *Firstborn of Venice: Vicenza in the Early Renaissance State.* Baltimore, 1988.

Guillerme, André, *The Age of Water: The Urban Environment in the North of France, A.D. 300–1800.* College Station, Tex., 1988.

Hale, John R. "Renaissance Armies and Political Control: The Venetian Providitorial System, 1509–1529." *Journal of Italian History* 2 (spring 1979), 11–31.

Heil, B. *Die deutschen Stadte und Burgen im Mittelalter.* Leipzig, 1921.

Herlihy, David. *Cities and Society in Medieval Italy.* London, 1980.

_____. *Medieval and Renaissance Pistoia: The Social History of an Italian Town, 1200–1430.* New Haven, 1967.

_____. *Pisa in the Early Renaissance: A Study of Urban Growth.* New Haven, 1958.

_____. "Population, Plague, and Social Change in Rural Pistoia, 1201–1430." *Economic History Review,* 2nd ser., 18 (1965), 225–244.

Herlihy, David, and Christiane Klapisch-Zuber. *Tuscans and Their Families: A Study of the Florentine Catasto of 1427.* New Haven, 1985.

Hoffmann, Richard C. "Fishing for Sport in Medieval Europe: New Evidence." *Speculum* 60 (October 1985), 877–902.

Hohenberg, Paul M., and Lynn Hollen Lees *The Making of Urban Europe, 1000–1950.* Cambridge, Mass., 1985.

Holmes, Urban T. *Daily Living in the Twelfth Century.* Madison, Wis., 1964.

Hughes, J. Donald. *Ecology in Ancient Civilizations.* Albuquerque, N. Mex., 1975.

_____. *Pan's Travail: Environmental Problems of the Ancient Greeks and Romans.* Baltimore, 1994.

Hyde, John Kenneth. *Padua in the Age of Dante.* New York, 1966.

_____. *Society and Politics in Medieval Italy: The Evolution of the Civil Life, 1000–1350.* Aylesbury, Great Britain, 1973.

Jepson, Henry Lorenzo. *The Sanitary Evolution of London.* Brooklyn, N.Y., 1907.

Jolowicz, Herbert Felix, and Barry Nicholas. *Historical Introduction to the Study of Roman Law.* 3d ed. Cambridge, 1972.

Jusserand, J. J., and Lucy Toulmen Smith. *English Wayfaring Life in the Middle Ages (XIVth Century).* 3d ed. Williamsburg, Mass., 1974.

Laduri, E. LeRoy. *Times of Feast and Times of Famine: A History of Climate Since the Year 1000.* New York, 1971.

Lanconelli, Angela. "Contratti agrari e rapporti di lavoro nell'Italia medievale." *Studi storici* 23 (July-September 1982), 639–646.

Lane, F. C. *Venice, a Maritime Republic.* Baltimore, 1973.

Leighton, Albert C. *Transport and Communications in Early Medieval Europe, A.D. 500–1100.* New York, 1972.

The Lombard Laws, ed. and trans. Katherine Fischer Drew. Philadelphia, 1973.

Lombardini, G. *Pane e denaro a Bassano tra il 1501 e il 1799.* Vicenza, 1963.

Luzzatto, Gino. *An Economic History of Italy from the Fall of the Roman Empire to the Beginning of the Sixteenth Century.* New York, 1961.

Macaulay, David. *City: A Story of Roman Planning and Construction.* Boston, 1974.

Martines, Lauro. *Power and Imagination: City-States in Renaissance Italy.* New York, 1979.

_____, ed. *Violence and Civil Disorder in Italian Cities, 1200–1500.* Berkeley, 1972.

Melosi, Martin V. *Garbage in the Cities: Refuse, Reform, and the Environment, 1880–1980.* College Station, Tex., 1981.

Menesto, Enrico. "Statuti rurali e statuti di valle (secoli XIII–XVIII). La provincia di Bergamo (Bergamo, 5 marzo 1983)." *Studi Medievali* 24 (1) (1983), 415–422.

Meroni, U. *Cremona fedelissima.* Cremona, 1951–1957.

Miskimin, Harry A., David Herlihy, and A. L. Udovitch. *The Medieval City.* New Haven, 1977.

Moore, Peter D. "Life Seen from a Medieval Latrine." *Nature* 294 (December 1981), 614.

Morgan, Morris Hicky, trans. *Vitruvius: The Ten Books on Architecture.* Reprint, New York, 1960.

Mumford, Lewis. *The City in History: Its Origins, Its Transformations, and Its Prospects.* New York, 1961.

Munro, Charles Henry, trans. *The Digest of Justinian.* 2 vols. Cambridge, 1904.

Murvar, Vatro, "Occidental Versus Oriental City." *Social Forces* 44 (3) (March 1966), pp. 384ff.

Neckam, Alexander. *Speculum Speculationum.* Oxford, 1988.

Noyes, Ella. *The Story of Ferrara.* Nendeln-Liechtenstein, 1970.

Ortalli, Gherardo. "Il ruolo degli statuti tra autonomie e dipendenze: Curzole e il dominio Veniceno." *Rivista Storica Italiana* 98 (1) (1986), 195–220.

Osheim, Duane J. "Country Men and the Law in Late-Medieval Tuscany." *Speculum* 64 (April 1989), 317–337.

_____. *An Italian Lordship: The Bishopric of Lucca in the Late Middle Ages.* Los Angeles, 1977.

_____. "Rural Population and the Tuscan Economy in the Late Middle Ages." *Viator* 7 (1976), 329–346.

Ovitt, George J. "The Cultural Context of Western Technology: Early Christian Attitudes Toward Manual Labor." *Technology and Culture* 27 (July 1986), 477–500.

Partner, Peter. *The Lands of St. Peter: The Papal State in the Middle Ages and the Early Renaissance.* Berkeley, 1972.

Pini, Antonio Ivan. "Potere pubblico e addetti ai transporti e al cetovagliamento cittadini nel Medioevo: Il caso di Bologna." *Nuova rivista storica* 66 (May–August 1982), 253–281.

Polsby, Nelson. *Community Power and Political Theory.* New Haven, 1983.

Postan, Michael M. *Essays on Medieval Agriculture and General Problems of the Medieval Economy.* Cambridge, 1973.

_____. "Investment in Medieval Agriculture." *Journal of Economic History* 27 (1967).

_____. *The Medieval Economy and Society: An Economic History of Britain in the Middle Ages.* Reprint, New York, 1984.

Rackham, Oliver. "Ancient Landscapes." In *The Greek City: From Homer to Alexander,* ed. Oswyn Murray and Simon Price. Oxford, 1990.

Raftis, J. A. "Ecological Dimensions of Medieval Agrarian Systems: A Medievalist Responds." *Agricultural History* 52 (October 1978), 484–487.

The Regimen of Health of the Medical School of Salerno, ed. and trans. Pascale P. Parente. New York, 1967.

Renna, Thomas. "The Idea of the City in Bernard of Clairvaux and Thomas Merton." *Michigan Academician* 15 (winter 1983), 241–252.

Renzi, Salvatore De. *Collectio Salernitana ossia Documenti inediti, e trattati Medicina appartenenti alla Scuola Medica Salernitana.* 4 vols. Naples, 1852–1856.

Reynolds, Reginald. *Cleanliness and Godliness, or the Further Metamorphosis of Ajax. . . .* Garden City, N.Y., 1946.

Reynolds, Robert L. *Europe Emerges: Transition Toward an Industrial World-Wide Society, 600–1750.* Madison, Wis., 1961.

Reynolds, Susan. "Law and Communities in Western Christendom c. 900–1140." *American Journal of Legal History* 25 (July 1981), 205–224.

Robbins, F. W. *The Story of the Land and the Candle.* London, 1939.

Rover, R. A. de. *The Rise and Decline of the Medici Bank, 1397–1494.* Cambridge, 1963.

Rorig, Fritz. *The Medieval Town.* Berkeley, 1967.

Rosen, George A. *A History of Public Health.* New York, 1958.

Rubinstein, N. "Some Ideas on Municipal Progress and Decline in the Italy of the Commune." In D. J. Gordon, ed., *Fritz Saxel.* London, 1957.

Saalman, Howard. *Medieval Cities.* New York, 1968.

Sabine, Ernest L. "Butchering in Medieval London." *Speculum* 8 (1933), 335–353.

_____. "City Cleaning in Medieval London." *Speculum* 12 (1937), 19–43.

_____. "Latrines and Cesspools of Medieval London." *Speculum* 9 (1934), pp. 303–321.

Scalvini, Maria Luisa, Gian Piero Calza, and Paola Finardi. *Bergamo.* Roma, 1987.

Sedgewick, Henry Dwight. *Italy in the Thirteenth Century.* Boston, 1933.

Sedgwick, William T. *Principles of Sanitary Science and the Public Health with Special Reference to the Causation and Prevention of Infectious Diseases.* New York, 1908.

Sestan, E. "La citta comunale italiana di secoli X–XII." In *XI Congres International des Sciences Historiques,* vol. 3. Stockholm, 1960.

Simon, John. *English Sanitary Institutions, Reviewed in Their Course of Development and in Some of Their Political and Social Relations.* London, 1970.

Singer, Charles, et al. *A History of Technology. Vol. 2, The Mediterranean Civilizations and the Middle Ages, c. 700 B.C. to c. A. D. 1500.* New York, 1956.

Slicher van Bath, B. H. *The Agrarian History of Western Europe, 500–1850.* London, 1963.

Storti Storchi, Claudia. *Diritto e istituzioni a Bergamo dal comune alla signoria.* Pubblicazioni dell'Istituto di storia del diritto otaliano, 10. Milan, 1984.

Strayer, Joseph R., and Dana C. Munro. *The Middle Ages, 395–1500.* 4th ed. New York, 1959.

Tabacco, Giovanni. *The Struggle for Power in Medieval Italy: Structures of Political Rule.* Cambridge, 1989.

Tabanelli, Mario. *Pandolfo III Malatesta, signore di Brescia e di Bergamo: Un condottiero Romegnolo in Lombardia.* Brescia, 1978.

Te Brake, William H. "Air Pollution and Fuel Crises in Pre-Industrial London, 1250–1650." *Technology and Culture* 16 (July 1975), 337–359.

Thomas, Joseph Anthony Charles. *Textbook of Roman Law.* New York, 1976.

Thorndike, Lynn. "Sanitation, Baths and Street Cleaning in the Middle Ages and Renaissance." *Speculum* 3 (1928), 192–203.

_____. "Sanitation in French Towns." *Speculum* 14 (1939), 272.

Ullmann, Walter. *The Growth of Papal Government in the Middle Ages: A Study in the Ideological Relation of Clerical to Lay Power.* Reprint, London, 1965.

_____. *The Medieval Idea of Law as Represented by Lucas de Penna: A Study in Fourteenth-Century Legal Scholarship.* London, 1946.

_____. *The Papacy and Political Ideas in the Middle Ages.* London, 1976.

Vecchi, Alberto. "I luoghi comuni nell-agiografia. Saggio sulla leggenda veronese di S. Zeno." *Augustinianum* 24 (August 1984), 143–166.

Waley, Daniel. *The Italian City-Republics.* Reprint, New York, 1978.

_____. *Medieval Orvieto: The Political History of an Italian City-State, 1157–1334.* Cambridge, 1952.

_____. *The Papal State in the Thirteenth Century.* London, 1961.

Weber, Max. *The City.* Glencoe, Ill., 1958.

_____. "Class, Status, Party." In *From Max Weber's Essays in Sociology,* ed. and trans. H. H. Gerth and C. Wright. New York, 1946.

_____. *Economy and Society: An Outline of Interpretive Sociology.* Berkeley, 1978.

_____. *General Economic History.* New York, 1961.

_____. *The Theory of Social and Economic Organization.* New York, 1947.

White, Lynn Townsend. *Medieval Technology and Social Change.* Oxford, 1962.

_____. *The Transformation of the Roman World: Gibbon's Problem After Two Centuries.* Berkeley, 1966.

Wiel, Althea. *The Story of Bologna.* Nendeln-Liechtenstein, 1970.

_____. *The Story of Verona.* Nendeln-Liechtenstein, 1971.

Williman, Daniel, ed. *The Black Death: The Impact of the Fourteenth-Century Plague.* Vol. 13. Binghamton, N.Y., 1982.

Yonge, C. M. "Fisheries in History: The Tunny, the Herring, and the Cod." *History Today* 25 (May 1975), 332–339.

Zanetti, D. *Problemi alimentari di una economia preindustriale.* Turin, 1964.

Zdekauer, Lodovico. "Statuti criminali del foro ecclesiastico di Siena." *Bulletino Senese di storia patria* 7 (1900), 231–264.

Ziegler, Philip. *The Black Death.* New York, 1971.

Modern Environmental Law

Arbuckle, J. Gordon, et al. *Environmental Law Handbook.* 12th ed. Rockville, Md., 1993.

Brenton, Tony. *The Greening of Machiavelli: The Evolution of International Environmental Politics.* London, 1994.

Caldwell, Lynton Keith. *International Environmental Policy: Emergence and Dimensions.* 2d ed. Durham, N.C., 1990.

Garbutt, J. H. *Environmental Law: A Practical Handbook.* London, 1992.

_____. *Waste Management Law: An Outline of Planning, Environmental, and Health and Safety Law.* London, 1992.

Garrett, Theodore L., ed. *The Enviromental Law Manual.* Chicago, 1992.

Grieves, Forest L. *International Law, Organization, and the Environment: A Bibliography and Research Guide.* Tucson, Ariz., 1974.

Handler, Thomas, ed. *Regulating the European Environment.* London, 1994.

Kasto, Jalil. *Modern International Law of the Environment.* Kingston, N. Y. 1995.

King, James J. *The Environmental Dictionary.* 2d ed. New York, 1993.

Kiss, Alexandre Charles. *International Environmental Law.* Ardsley-on-Hudson, N.Y., 1991.

_____. *Manual of European Environmental Law.* New York, 1993.

Kubasek, Nancy. *Environmental Law.* Englewood Cliffs, N.J., 1994.

Mackenthun, Kenneth Marsh. *Environmental Regulations Handbook.* Boca Raton, Fla., 1992.

Molitor, Michael R., ed. *International Environmental Law: Primary Materials.* Deventer, Netherlands, 1991.

Murphy, Earl Finbar. *Man and His Environment: Law.* New York, 1971.

Rogers, William H. *Handbook on Environmental Law.* St. Paul, 1977.

Smith, Turner T. *Understanding European Environmental Regulation.* New York, 1993.

Teclaff, Ludwik A., ed. *International Environmental Law.* New York, 1974.

Templeton, Virginia Evans. *World Environment Law Bibliography.* Littleton, Colo., 1987.

Weiss, Edith Brown. *International Environmental Law: Basic Instruments and References.* Dobbs Ferry, N.Y., 1992.

About the Book and Authors

The history of the medieval towns of northern and central Italy opens a window onto the concerns of urban elites throughout the medieval world regarding the environment and quality of life. In *Straws in the Wind,* the authors demonstrate that legislative efforts to control the environment were neither haphazard nor accidental. Rather, they were rational responses to perceived needs, often based on a valuable store of knowledge inherited from their Roman forebears.

Zupko and Laures describe who these early environmentalists were, what motivated them, how they shaped the environmental programs they devised, and how they implemented and enforced these regulations. The book examines the efforts of town officials, often acting independently of powerful regional, papal, and imperial authorities, to provide their citizens with the best possible urban quality of life—within the limits of their knowledge, experience, and technology. Moreover, Zupko and Laures reveal evidence of grassroots support for the protection of resources and for the preservation of air, water, and the aesthetic qualities of the urban environment. The results of these efforts, when compared to those of the modern environmental movement, were very modest, merely "straws in the wind." Nonetheless, they were the harbingers of the future.

Ronald E. Zupko is professor of history at Marquette University. **Robert A. Laures** is a medieval historian living in Milwaukee, Wisconsin.

Index